FAITH IN THE FUTURE

CHRISTIAN INVOLVEMENT IN SHAPING OUR SOCIETY

A STUDY GUIDE

Written by Elizabeth Breuilly,
Celia Deane-Drummond
and Martin Palmer of ICOREC.

© The International Consultancy on Religion, Education and Culture 1991.

All rights reserved.

First published in Great Britain in 1991 by HarperCollins Ltd,
77 – 85 Fulham Palace Road, Hammersmith, London W6.

Cartoons by Fran Orford of Fran Orford Cartoons.

Design by Caro Inglis.

Typesetting by Point·2·Point, Whaley Bridge

Printed and bound by H. Shanley, Bolton

Printed on recycled paper.

ISBN 0 00 599294 X

ACKNOWLEDGMENTS

Our thanks go in particular to the following organisations and individuals without whose assistance this book would not have been possible.

British Gas PLC. The Malvern Conference, to which much of this book relates, was funded in the major part by British Gas PLC, as part of its programme of community involvement.

The Bishop of Worcester and William Temple, Archbishop of Canterbury (1942 – 44). The inspiration for this book and the accompanying radio series came as a tribute to the genius of Archbishop William Temple, who, in the dark days of 1941 called the first Malvern Conference to plan for a new future for Britain. In 1991, Philip Goodrich, Bishop of Worcester had the vision to call Malvern II, to look at Britain's role in Europe and the world.

World Wide Fund for Nature UK. WWF UK, through its Network on Conservation and Religion assisted in the funding of both the Malvern Conference 91 and the book. The team of writers from ICOREC were also funded by WWF as part of their contribution to a wider involvement of the churches in environmental and associated issues.

BBC Radio 4. Noel Vincent and Jackie Barnett of BBC North, who worked long hours to make it possible for the radio series to reflect and enhance the study book.

Finally, to all at the Malvern Conference 91 who gave of their time, insights and energies, especially Owen Nankivell, John Bell and colleagues from the Iona community for the worship and the many who gave so generously of their time.

To accompany this study book, the BBC has produced five programmes in their series *Seeds of Faith*. These are broadcast for five Sunday nights from November 24th to the 22nd December 1991 at 11.30 p.m. A cassette of the programmes for use with this book is available from:

Noel Vincent,
BBC Religious Broadcasting,
New Broadcasting House,
P.O. Box 27,
Oxford Road,
Manchester M60 1SJ.

Please send a cheque or postal order for £3.99 made out to BBC North, along with your name and address. The price includes post and packaging.

CONTENTS

MAKING BEST USE OF THIS BOOK

Welcome to the study book *Faith in the Future*. This has been designed for use by individuals wishing to explore more deeply the relationship between the Christian faith and pressing issues of today: for church study groups – maybe a Lent House group; and for schools, especially for General Studies and for certain sections of the GCSE Religious Education syllabus.

The book has arisen from studies undertaken across the spectrum of Christian denominations in the UK. It is a truly ecumenical venture as well as having been able to draw upon many people within the specialist fields discussed in the main chapters. We are very grateful for all the assistance we have had from different groups and individuals, too numerous to mention by name.

The material in each chapter will more than fill an evening discussion group! Therefore we suggest that any group leader or teacher look through the main chapters (2-6) in order to decide which aspect of the issues explored would be best for the group to discuss. Each chapter could in fact provide enough material for a set of meetings.

Within each chapter there are a series of discussion pointers, possible activities and projects. They are included to assist both the individual reader in terms of looking anew at certain issues or activities, and especially for the group leader or teacher.

The Radio 4 series of five support programmes is available on cassette. Each programme has been designed to offer further insights and views from a wide cross section of people, on the issues raised in the five main chapters. If you are using it with a group or class, we suggest playing the tape and then using the discussion questions and appropriate materials from the study book.

While the heart of the issues is to be found in the five main chapters (2-6), we have also provided an opening chapter on the nature of Christian faith today and a final chapter which projects that faith into the future. While the final chapter can be used for follow up, we strongly urge that all groups look at the major theological points raised in chapter one, before starting on the more specific social issues of the rest of the book.

Finally, there is a short bibliography of books easily available, for those interested in going more deeply into the subjects raised.

Martin Palmer/Circa Photo Library

FAITH IN GOD

Hope for the Future

When St. Matthew came to end his Gospel, he did so with a beautiful but at the same time, demanding vision of the future. He tells of Jesus sending his followers out to make disciples of all nations, to baptise them in the name of the Father, the Son and the Holy Spirit, to teach them the ways of God and to follow in the way of Jesus himself. Finally, Jesus gave them the great promise:

> "And know that I am with you always: yes, even to the end of time."

(Matthew 28:20)

This promise that Jesus will be with us whatever happens and until the end of time has sustained Christians down through the centuries. It is still our hope today. But what relevance can the Christian faith in God have for the social, political and environmental issues which confront us all today? What has economics, the arts, the media, to do with our salvation through Jesus Christ? Christians understand God to be at work in the world through the Holy Trinity – Father, Son and Holy Spirit. To help us begin to understand this, listen to this new exploration of the meaning of the Trinity.

> "Glory be to God,
> Architect and Innovator,
> Creator of all from nothing,
> Source of power,
> Parent of humanity,
> who, though wrapped round with
> the majesty of heaven,
> bends down for the people of earth.

> Glory be to God.

> Glory be to Jesus Christ,
> Carpenter, storyteller,
> Healer, Debater,
> Companion of the dispossessed,
> Troubler of the powerful,

who, though able to put right the world by decree,
saves it by suffering.

Glory be to Christ.

Glory be to the Holy Spirit,
Inspirer and Disturber,
Breath of life,
Midwife of change,
Revealer of hidden truth,
Lamplighter,
who, though present throughout creation,
is particularly close to us here.

Glory be to the Spirit."

This prayer to the Trinity was composed for the opening act of worship at the Malvern 91 Conference, called to explore the relationship between Christian faith and the major issues that confront us today. This engagement will also give us clues to the future. In this study book, we look at the pressing issues which confront us in our own country, as a more active member of Europe and in the world. We do so in the light of our belief in the redeeming power of the Father, Son and Holy Spirit.

---

1. Spend time in the group meditating on the prayer above – the Trinity prayer. Talk about about what it says to you. Add to it as a group if you wish.
2. We suggest you pray the Trinity prayer as an introduction or closing to each of your study sessions.

William Temple and Malvern 41

In 1941, the then Archbishop of York (later of Canterbury) William Temple, called a conference of church leaders and others such as T.S. Eliot the poet, to discuss what sort of society Britain should be working towards, after the war. The vision of a more just society, within which people's basic needs were met, helped to lay the foundation stone for the welfare state which emerged after the war. In 1942 William Temple published a popular book which captured his ideas on Christian involvement in society, entitled *Christianity and the Social Order*. This book, with its vision of Christianity providing the basic moral and ethical foundations for a fair society, influenced many in their thinking about both the faith and the future. He made it clear that the primary Christian principles which should inform any discussion are faith in God the creator, and the belief in the dignity of every human being. The practical consequences of this belief offered guidelines for society in terms of, for example, adequate housing for all and the right of all workers to have education and holidays, in a way that found echoes later in the formulation of the welfare state. He also made it clear in this book that he endorsed an idealistic vision of the church. He believed that the church could lift the difficulties encountered in society to a new plane where any difficulties disappeared. He hoped to set theological principles alongside particular problems, so that they could find solutions to these problems in the middle ground between them.

But much has changed since 1941 and William Temple's vision has proved to be harder than many expected. It proved very difficult to link the guidelines offered by the church to particular concrete decisions in particular circumstances. Indeed, some would now claim that such a vision of the role of the church is impossible and was wrong in the first place. The social advances which were made after the war have been suffering both from loss of vision and from some who have attacked the very idea of the welfare state. The assumption of a public good has been shaken by the rise of self-righteous self-interest, as typified in the yuppie culture of the eighties. Christianity seems to have lost its place as the accepted faith of Britain, as secularism and the rise of other faith communities has eroded its traditional position. The rise of the professional carers, such as social workers, psychiatrists and advice bureaus has made the caring role of the Church seem marginal.

In looking to the future as Christians living in a Britain which is now more and more involved in Europe, we need to be aware of a very interesting shift. In the 19th century, Western Christianity seemed on the brink of taking over the world. Missions had reached virtually every corner of the world. Other faiths seemed to be in retreat before the onslaught of the Gospel. Western political power controlled vast swathes of the world and seemed to offer both support for the Gospel and evidence that the people of the Gospel were in charge of the world. Triumphalism – the idea that Christianity and the West had triumphed over all foes – was the attitude of the West, of both Church and society. What could stop the ultimate victory of the Gospel?

Two World Wars, the Holocaust, the revelation of the brutality of imperialism and the collapse of belief in 'progress' have dealt a near fatal blow to the Church's idea that Christianity was going to triumph in the world. Christians have learnt some humility. The revival of other faiths, most notably Islam, Hinduism and Buddhism and their arrival in our own societies, has led to a reevaluation of the place of Christianity. While some have lost faith in Christianity and others still wish to claim it will 'triumph', many have come to realise that Christianity does not equal Western civilisation. The need for the Gospel to be able to speak in all cultures and through a variety of means, has meant that the old assumption that Christianity equals the West has either gone or is no longer seriously considered by many Christians.

However, triumphalism is far from dead in other sectors of European society. Living at this extraordinary time of the collapse of the Soviet Communist system and its client states, we also live in a time of a certain kind of Western triumphalism. It is perhaps best captured in the odd but thought provoking statement by the American historian Francis Fukiyama that with the collapse of the other great ideological system, Western free enterprise and democracy has won and thus history has ended! By this, Fukiyama means that history is usually about the clash of cultures. Now that there is only one culture in the world – Western capitalism and democracy – history is over!

In many discussions about the fate of Eastern Europe, it is hard not to detect a triumphalism in the voices and attitudes of the statesmen and business leaders of the West. If the Eastern block wishes to join us, then they can wait until we decide we want them, until they reach our level of consumerist democracy. We, after all, are the victors, so we set the conditions. This is taken up further in chapter 3.

The Church, having itself played this game of triumphalism, needs to sound warnings about secular triumphalism. In the West we may well have the toughest and possibly the most workable political and economic system in the world. Yet it damages and discards many thousands of people every year through poverty, unemployment, inequality and even at times oppression. Its values are literally eating up the world and destroying much which we need and the rest of the planet needs for survival. Our system of democracy has in some places become distorted into little more than promises of more and more material goods as a bribe for people to give their votes. This has been acknowledged in Roman Catholic documents such as the Papal Encyclical *Centesimus Annus* which openly talks about the crisis in democracy.

This crisis in democracy means that the powerless remain powerless and greater and greater financial power comes to rest in the hands of the banks and the major companies. While some of these are recognising their duties to society as well as their trading relations with society, these remain the exception not the rule. Increasingly we have become a society in which the experts – economists, politicians, scientists and so on – have taken control away from ordinary people and communities.

What does the Christian faith have to say or offer to such a world?

3. In what ways have your local area, Britain and the world changed within your memory? Depending on the age and experience of the group, choose a period within the last 50 years, and write a dialogue between someone living then and someone living now. Draw out as many differences as you can: in politics, faith, invention, discoveries, attitudes, etc.

4. What were your reactions and hopes in 1989 when you heard that the Berlin Wall was breached? What are your feelings now about developments in Eastern Europe?

5. Read Luke 18:9-14. As a group, re-write the story with modern characters. The 'Pharisee' need not necessarily be priding him or herself on religious matters, but on anything you think is relevant.

6. Christians naturally want to celebrate God's glory and goodness, but this can sometimes become triumphalism. Write a modern-day psalm, celebrating God's goodness in a way that is not triumphalist.

Crisis of Confidence

In the years since 1941, the Church in Britain has been through a major crisis of confidence. Its hopes for a more just society seemed to be fulfilled at first, but soon the perhaps oversimplified vision of a Christian Socialist future began to falter as problems arose for which the Church seemed unable to offer any clear answer.

In the 1960's this crisis was reflected in a public challenging of the relevance not just of the Church to social issues, but of the Church's teachings themselves. Numbers coming to Church dropped dramatically in all denominations. Falling congregations found themselves inhabiting echoing vast churches which they could never fill. Old certainties seemed to be overthrown almost overnight and all forms of authority – including the Church – were challenged in a very radical way. The effect was to disorientate many Christians. Some felt that it was vital to strip the Gospel of all elements which were not 'down to earth'. It was felt that if we could get rid of all the supernatural elements of the

Bible and of the faith, then this would speak more clearly to secular society. In reaction to this, others sought to become even more closely wedded to Biblical language and imagery and the seeds of a rise in fundamentalism were sown. Within traditional structures like the Roman Catholic Church, some challenged the Church to change, while others were distressed when changes did happen.

Protestant theologian Ted Peters says:

> "Most of today's clergy were trained at a time when we in the Church believed the world around us had forsaken things religious. We thought the world view of natural science would soon eradicate religion from the Western world. We were taught in seminary that our preaching and teaching had to become 'relevant' to the modern world, and this meant the *secular* world. If the Christianity we were going to teach was to be relevant, then it needed to shed its offensive religious trappings."

> *The Cosmic Self, (Ted Peters. Harper, San Francisco 1991.)*

Others reacted by turning their backs on the rising tides of different ideas, causes and concerns which came to the fore in the 1960's. They took refuge in old certainties such as the Bible and tradition and ignored the changes around them. For some, the very unrelatedness of the Gospel to contemporary society stood as a sign that society was wrong.

In both cases, what was happening was the same. There was a failure of Christian nerve, a feeling that Christianity was no longer intimately at the heart of our society and thus close to the great issues of the day and their resolution. Christianity was having a major crisis of confidence in itself and tended to split into two camps: the evangelicals/traditionalists and the liberal/social concern wing.

Since the 1960's both of these trends have continued but much has also grown up between them. Now it is not at all unusual to find deeply committed evangelical Christians equally deeply involved in anti-racist work; in providing training for the unemployed; in movements for changing international economics or struggling for the environment. Likewise, many committed social action Christians find great help in spiritual retreats, in new worship and in the rediscovery of the mystical and narrative within Christianity. In Roman Catholicism, the great changes brought about the Second Vatican Council in the mid-60's has meant an increasing emphasis on social concern as part of the mission of the Church.

The acceptance that Britain is now a pluralist society – composed of many different groups with their own beliefs and values – is held right across the Church. Some on the extremes of the Church feel this is either nothing but good, or at the other extreme, nothing but bad. But most Christians would agree with the evangelical writer Canon Christopher Lamb:

> "Western society is now irretrievably mixed, pluralist in character. This has happened partly because of the breakdown of a single world-view, a process beginning many centuries ago . . . For myself, as a Christian, I see great testing and therefore great value for Christian understanding in the painful sifting process brought about by religious and cultural pluralism. For too long religion has been identified in the European mind with Christianity. For too long, in consequence, morality and Christian faith have been thought to be the same thing, so that 'preaching' is dismissed as telling others to be good, and 'the decent person' thought to be the real Christian."

Belief in a Mixed Society, (Christopher Lamb, Lion. 1985.)

Turn to questions
on next page

7. Can Britain be described as a Christian country today? In what ways is British society Christian, and in what ways is it not?

8. Is the rest of Europe any different in this respect? Be as specific as you can, and pool any experience or knowledge that you have in the group about other European countries.

9. What do people who are not Christians want from the Church?

10. What are the most important things the Church has to offer to today's society in Britain, in Europe and in the world?

a) As a group, make as large a list as you can.

b) Now imagine that you are in charge of all the money that Christians give, and all the time they give. Make two piecharts, one for time and one for money, showing how you think these should be allocated.

Discuss these charts and keep them safe. You might refer to them at the end of your *Faith in the Future* study.

Having faith to speak and act

The vision of the Trinity which is given at the beginning of this chapter seems to capture something of the emerging new vision of Christianity in relationship to the wider world. It is becoming increasingly clear that a 'secular society' doesn't mean that people have given up the quest for the religious. Far from it. As 'secular society' seems to be reaching out for almost anything which claims to be religious or spiritual, the Church is felt to have little to offer, and seems almost to have thrown out the spiritual baby with the bath water. In the rush of some Christians to be relevant, we have sometimes forgotten the eternal nature of the truths our faith has: that God loves, Christ heals and the Spirit renews. In the frightened retreat by some Christians from engaging with the social woes of our world, we have forgotten that

TIME

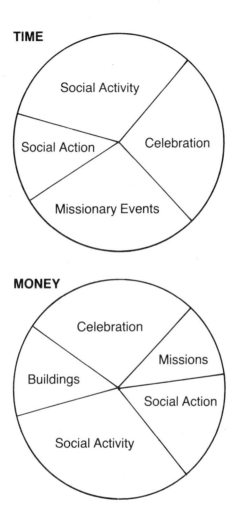

Social Activity

Social Action

Celebration

Missionary Events

MONEY

Celebration

Missions

Buildings

Social Action

Social Activity

Jesus gave us a clear picture of what his wish was for Christian social life, in the parable of the Sheep and Goats in Matthew 25 and the Beatitudes in Matthew 5.

The rediscovery of the relevance of Christian language and beliefs to a society which is looking for both material and spiritual responses to its ills and concerns came out very clearly when the fiftieth anniversary of Malvern 1941 was celebrated. Throughout the conference, called to discuss the role of Christianity in Britain, in Britain in Europe and in Europe in the world, the need to root ourselves in a proper Christian and therefore theological basis was expressed. In particular, it was felt that we needed a firmer theology of Creation. What should it mean to us to confess, as the Nicene Creed expresses:

"We believe in one God, the Father, the Almighty, maker of heaven and earth, of all that is, seen and unseen."

---

11. Read Genesis 1. What does it mean to you to say that human beings are made 'in the image of God'? To help you

a) look back at the Trinity prayer on page 12

b) ' . . . the Church affirmed clearly and forcefully that every individual – whatever his or her personal convictions – bears the image of God and therefore deserves respect.'

(Centesimus Annus)

12. Begin a list of words and phrases which describe the image of God in us. Add to this list as you work through the Study Guide.

However, we also need to hold up the figure of the suffering Christ and of the empty tomb. In a world where certainty has so often led to disaster – be that religious certainty which has given us Northern Ireland and countless other wars which have religious roots, or ideological certainty such as Soviet Communism and its terrors – we need to show that at the heart of our vision for the world is a paradox. The God of Love, suffering on a cross: the death and burial of hope which springs forth again on the third day: the lowly raised up high; the Source of All emptying himself to live with the poor and the dispossessed. In all the issues which we shall study in greater detail in the following chapters, we shall need to encounter the Christ paradox – the scandal of hope hung upon a cross, the joy of death being overcome. Without this ability to look for and seek to find the image of Christ in our troubled world, we shall fail to understand the true context of our God-given powers of creativity.

We also need to look for signs of that Spirit which hovered over the waters at the Creation; which stirred the hearts and minds of the terrified disciples at Pentecost and which is at work in the world. Thank God, the work of the Holy Spirit is not limited by the Church. Learning in humility to see and be encountered by the Holy Spirit in places and people we would not expect, is also part of the way into the future for Christians.

WHOSE SOCIETY IS IT ANYWAY?

CITIZENSHIP AND RESPONSIBILITY

Of peoples and nations

Where do we belong? At one level this might seem quite an easy question to answer. We belong with our family, our church or local community. But where are our roots? How many of you still live in the area where you were born and where your parents were born? For those who do not live in such a place, where do we feel is 'home'? Is it where you grew up? Where you spent your summers? Where your parents live?

The question of where we belong is an increasingly important one as Britain becomes more fully part of Europe. There are many who fear that becoming 'European' will mean that we shall lose our sense of identity. The fear is that being part of something so big and unspecific will mean we will feel homeless or rootless.

The communities of Jesus

The story of Jesus's birth gives us a clue as to the Christian understanding of identity and community. In chapter 2 of St. Luke's Gospel, we are told where Jesus fitted in to the wider and local community of his time. This rooting of Jesus in time and place is central to the Christian claim that God in Christ was truly incarnate and really lived amongst us. St. Luke tells us that Jesus was born as part of the Roman Empire under Caesar Augustus; that he lived in the Roman province of Syria while Quirinius was governor; that his family lived in Nazareth in the district of Galilee; that Jesus was of the family line of King David and that the 'home' of David's line was Bethlehem. There is no doubt in anyone's mind that Jesus is Jewish, comes from the House of David, has his family home in Nazareth, lives in Syria and is part of the Roman Empire. Jesus is at once rooted by Luke in the key communities which will shape and give meaning to his life and ministry.

We all live in something of the same sort of world. Do you recall writing your address as a child? The usual format was to fill in that space on the Exercise Book which said 'Address' with something like this:

Fred Roots, Hartcliffe School, Hartcliffe, Bristol, England, the UK, Europe, the World, the Universe!

In a small way, it was exactly what St. Luke did in opening his account of the life of Jesus. He set Jesus in context and indicated the communities to which he belonged and where he was to exercise his responsibilities as a citizen of his time, faith and location.

The Celtic peoples and the UK

In 1707, the Act of Union formally created the United Kingdom by legally uniting Scotland with England, Wales and Ireland. This Union was created at the insistence of the stronger country, England, and against the wishes of many in Scotland. The Union was strongly opposed for many years in Scotland, Wales and Ireland. The Jacobite rebellion of Bonnie Prince Charlie in 1745, for example, was an attempt to shake off the heavy hand of England. After the defeat of Prince Charles at Culloden, there were widespread attempts to suppress Scottish identity and language. Gaelic was forbidden; kilts could not be worn and clans were forcibly removed from their traditional lands. In part these succeeded and, for instance, Gaelic is now only spoken by a handful of people in Scotland. But Scottish identity survived and is flourishing. The calls for a separate Assembly for Scotland reflect the strength of feeling about Scottish identity and power. Yet this is all taking place within the continued framework of the United Kingdom. Similarly, in Wales, weekend cottages have been set alight by Welsh nationalist extremists.

The tensions between the dominant culture of the UK and the Celtic groups, such as the Scots, are mirrored throughout Europe and throughout the world. We have watched with horror the struggles between Kurdish identity and Iraqi identity. We know that the Basques have, at times, taken to terrorist tactics in Spain to press home their claims for greater autonomy. In Brazil, the claims of the indigenous peoples of the Amazon are only now beginning to be heard – and for many of these groups it is too late. This century, above all centuries, has been marked by the attacks of majority groups upon minority groups; of culture against culture. In Germany, the Nazis and the Jews; in Russia, the Communists against the Church; in East Timor, the Indonesians against the Timorese – the list is long and tragic. It is no wonder that minority communities feel under threat from majority cultures. They are.

The UK is a good example of how minority cultures can survive but in a precarious way. Celtic identity – Welsh, Irish, Scottish and Cornish – is still part of the tapestry of British culture. In some places it is strong enough to be the predominant culture, as with the Welsh language in certain parts of Wales. But it is not really taken seriously within the wider culture of the UK. Minority cultural identity is taken as being in some degree good for a joke, but not for much else. Yet this identity still exists and persists.

Staying with the question of Celtic identity in the UK, most people from such cultures are not wanting to break up the UK. Nor do they wish to withdraw from being involved in Europe or in the wider world community. What they want is for their own identity to be seen as being a valid part of the wider community. They want protection and opportunities to ensure that their culture can survive, can contribute and can respond to the new challenges and opportunities which emerge as communities form and grow.

Inventing nations and dividing peoples

Often minority groups cut across what are now nation states. The Basques are to be found in both Spain and France; the Kurds live in the area which now forms parts of Turkey, Iraq, Iran and Syria. In Africa, the Europeans established boundaries for countries such as Uganda and Kenya which cut tribal lands in half and put the same peoples on either side of national boundaries. This serves to remind us that the idea of 'nation states' is quite a recent one. The emergence of nation states in Europe is in part the result of the collapse of the older concept of Christendom, focused upon the Holy Roman Empire. With the breakdown of the idea of a Christian Europe linked by faith, language (Latin) and loyalty to the Pope, the power vacuum was filled by national aspirations which gave us the political map of European nations which finally took shape after the creation of Germany and Italy in the late 19th century.

Wider afield, the vast majority of nation states in places such as South America, Central America, Africa and South East Asia, have arisen as a result of European power politics. Loyalties to such nations are often
still at variance with religious loyalties or community loyalties which

precede the formation of the these states. For example, the civil war in the Sudan has much to do with the desire of the Muslim north to be faithful to its ancient Islamic roots, while the South of the country wishes to form a Christian state. The attempt to keep them together within one, created, nation state has proved disastrous to all the peoples of that area.

The intervention of the West in vast areas of the world through trade and empire lies at the heart of the newer religious and ethnic communities in our societies – especially in the UK and other countries of Western Europe. Through colonial links and the need for cheap labour, large numbers of people from Africa, Asia, India and South America now form a part of our society. The diversity of beliefs, values and lifestyles they have brought have radically changed the nature of society in many places. The racism, prejudice and at times extreme violence these communities experience at the hands of some in our society raises uncomfortable questions about what sort of society we are, and what sort of society we will become. Can we find a place for such diversity within a greater community, or are we likely to fragment along sectarian lines? What does being British mean to children, Muslim, Christian or atheist, growing up in our communities today?

We have to beware of seeing the nation state as being the logical structure to which we should owe allegiance. Christians in particular know themselves to be members of a wider fellowship than just that of their nation state, yet Christianity also sees us taking seriously the variety of communities within which we live.

Turn to questions on next page

1.   People have a sense of belonging at many different levels: family, church, club, town or village, faith, country etc.

     List the four most important units that define what you are and where you belong. Try to put them in order of importance to you. Discuss the lists you have drawn up.

2.   What is the largest unit that you genuinely feel you belong to?

Living locally, thinking globally

One of the challenges to the Church is to help people find their place within both the local and the international communities – a case of living locally, thinking globally, an idea which some feel is summed up in the concept of subsidiarity. This term subsidiarity, means that decisions should be taken at the smallest or most local level possible, but within a framework which means that the concerns and interests of the wider community are also acknowledged. What it does not mean, or should not mean, is local self-centredness, which leads to a struggle for the selfish exercise of local concerns with no wider concern for the communities beyond. What is known in the environmental world as Nimby – Not In My Back Yard!

The Church offers a model of living locally, thinking globally. As members of our local denomination, we are part of a UK and world wide denomination. As local Christians of a given area, we are also part of the world wide Church of God – and we know that in most places, we will be welcomed to worship and fellowship by our fellow Christians. In recent years, there have been attempts to dissolve the different specific identities of various churches. Certain foolish barriers, unnecessary divisions and petty feuds have been resolved. But in the end people have recognised the need to have something which is of their own tradition, of their own area or region, to bring to the wider family of the Church. Most people no longer look to the ecumenical movement to produce one uniform church. We now look to see how, as Christians from diverse traditions and locations, we can work side by side with other Christians with their own traditions in doing the will of God in the world.

Such a model is one which Europe, as it moves towards greater social, political and economic unity, needs to have in mind. The rise of a more united Europe must not be at the expense of local culture and identity. At the Malvern Conference 91, this was expressed very forcefully. There were some who saw nothing for the minority cultures to fear in a more united Europe. Both Edward Heath and Lord Jenkins of Hillhead poured cold water on the idea that a bigger Europe meant the loss of local identity. It is very unlikely that the British and the French for instance, will ever become carbon copies of each other.

But there was very real fear from others. The Scots in particular wanted to stress that while many of them were very positive about Europe, they wanted to ensure that there was space and place for them, as Scots, to make a distinct contribution to the wider community. The question is, can this be done?

It is not just in Europe that such issues arise. In many parts of the world, this issue of the the minority and the majority is a matter of life and death. A classic example of this is the Yanomamo people of the Amazon. Isolated for centuries, their contact with the outside world since the late 50's has been disastrous for them. They have been hunted down, stricken with previously unencountered illnesses and dispossessed of their lands. The result has been the almost total extinction of the Yanomamo. In what may well be their epitaph, one of their leaders has summed up the nature of the clash or encounter between minority and majority cultures:

> "Everyone likes to give as well as to receive. No-one wishes only to receive all the time. We have taken much from your culture . . . I wish you had taken something from our culture . . . for there were some good and beautiful things in it."

The need for us to find a proper balance between the local, regional, national and international is vital. We cannot live as though other communities do not exist. The world has become too small for that. However, we cannot play a part in this wider world unless we feel confident and secure in our own identity. The Helsinki Statement on Human Rights offers a powerful model for the sort of inter-relationship that should exist between local cultures and the wider political society, be that nation state, European community or world community:

> "National identity is a vital part of human identity and we claim it as a right to be recognised both culturally and politically. We reject aggressive nationalism based on exclusive theories of race, language and religious identity. We affirm within the unity of Europe the diverse identities of all its peoples"

Being Responsible – but to whom and for what?

If we can begin to answer where we belong, we then have to ask the next question. Who are we responsible to and for what are we responsible? In the model of citizenship which most countries in Europe assume, we are responsible for our own country. In a wider Europe, we are expected to also share our responsibilities to some degree with peoples of other countries. But where do we really feel our responsibilities lie?

For some people, it does not seem to go much beyond the family. If you have ever been out doing door-to-door collection for a charity such as Christian Aid, you will know how often people's sense of responsibility seems to stop at their front door! For others, it is the local community – perhaps the school or the church or local environmental issues. For others, it is the political parties or national trades unions or the company they work for. They feel a responsibility to these communities. For others it is the world wide community of Christians, of workers, of the poor, of the multi-nationals. For many people it is a fusion of something of all of these, from the family to the international. But how do we know which should have our greatest loyalty – what should we be most responsible for?

> **3.** Look again at the list you made on page 30. For each identity or group you belong to, write down:
> **a)** what you gain from it
> **b)** what you give to it
> **c)** why you belong to it. Do you, or did you, have a choice?

Jesus and responsibility

Jesus offers us a picture of how our visions need to be constantly challenged; our sense of responsibility ever widened. In Jesus we meet, as the Prayer of the Trinity states at the beginning of chapter 1, the 'Companion of the dispossessed'. Take the account of the healing of the daughter of the Syro-Phenician woman in Matthew 15: 21 to 28. As a Syro-Phenician, the woman who came begging Jesus to heal her daughter, was not Jewish. She was a Gentile, or as some translations put it, a Canaanite one of the ancient enemies of Israel. Jesus at first appears to refuse to help her saying that he has been sent to the 'lost sheep of the House of Israel'. Yet the woman manages to show that she is as much a child of God as are the Jews. She illustrates that Jesus's ministry is to all those whose heavenly parent is God, not just to the House of Israel. Jesus has responsibility beyond the national and religious confines within which he had grown up.

If Jesus apparently needed reminding of his wider resonsibility, then it is no wonder that we often need such reminding! This is especially true in Britain and in Europe. Our own society or societies within Europe seem to have enough problems of their own without having to worry about others. There is a temptation to create a 'Fortress Europe' mentality – a defensive wall of trade barriers, currency differences and social legislation which ensures that those outside relatively prosperous Western Europe are kept outside. This is especially true with regard to Eastern Europe. While the 'West' rejoices at the collapse of the old totalitarian order, it is being more cautious about responding to the aspirations of the newly liberated societies of Eastern Europe. The European Community is setting very clear boundaries upon both the movement of people from Eastern Europe and the speed with which the countries can join the European Community.

Responsibility at international level

Here there is probably a major clash between the way Christianity understands the word 'community' and the way that the European Community understands the word. For Christians, community means relationships which extend beyond the economic or political into relationships of trust, of mutual assistance, of cooperation and of the struggle for a more just society. To many outside the European Community, the idea of Community it espouses seems to consist of a community of the well off protecting what they have. This 'Fortress Europe' mentality is one which needs to be challenged, and not just with regard to the rest of Europe. The message which goes out from gatherings such as the Group of Seven (G7) industrialised nations (USA, Japan, Britain, Italy, Germany, France and Canada) in their annual meetings is that they are concerned only with their own well-being. The sight of Mr. Gorbachev coming cap in hand to the G7 asking for financial help is one which captures well the sense of power and control which these industrialised nations exude. They seem to act as if their vision of what should be is the only vision; their understanding of reality, economic or political, the only reality. Through a sense of triumph and success, they appear closed to the ideas and hopes of others – not just others outside their community, but those within. Those who have not benefited from the structures which such communities have built – the poor, the unemployed, the marginalised. This is why the model of interaction between the major power blocks and the local community is so important. Without it, how can the voices of those who suffer or who have a better way forward, ever be heard?

Responsibility for our past

We in the West also have a responsibility to listen to the past. Many would argue that until we have realised the extent to which we have lived globally and thought locally, we shall not be able to understand the nature of our responsibilites for the present state of the world. In the not too distant past, Europe physically controlled much of the rest of the world. We ruled globally but thought and behaved locally in that much of the natural wealth of the other countries was brought to

Europe and enabled Europe to establish its industrial and financial muscle. In the process we often destroyed communities, disrupted relationships and eroded the natural environment. Europe has a legacy of guilt which it has to take responsibility for and which it needs to acknowledge. As a result of our imperial past, we have responsibilities for the present and future which we need to take on board. We still have unequal relationships with many countries in the Third World and we still benefit from their resources in a way which diminishes their possibilities of caring for their own people.

As such, one of the responsibilities of the Church to our nation, to Europe and to such bodies as the Group of Seven is to expose and discuss this past. We need to understand what our cultures have done to so many other cultures and communities of the world. Then we need to understand the nature of God's forgiveness which we are offered through Jesus Christ. It is not a forgiveness which leaves us free to continue to do what we were doing only more carefully. It is forgiveness which liberates us from the past by calling us to take responsibility for that past, for the future and to create new relationships with those against whom we have sinned.

To be forgiven by those whom our culture has robbed and abused, we need to learn how to ask for forgiveness from such communities. For instance, the United Church of Canada recently held a service of repentance when it asked for forgiveness for its past actions as part of the culture which crushed and destroyed so many of the cultures of the indigenous peoples of North America. From this action of public repentance, it has been possible for the Church and the indigenous peoples to work on a new relationship, a new set of mutual responsibilities. We need to look to such a new understanding between Europe and many of the other countries of the world. In the light of our realisation that we have been at the root of many of the problems encountered by other communities, we can start to see where we now need to go in terms of new relationships and fellowships. This may well at times bring us into conflict with other groups' ideas of community. And this raises the question of the responsibility of Christians to their government and of the government to God.

4. Think of some specific ways in which you can live locally and think globally. Can your church help you do this?

5. How far do you feel responsible for actions which you have no control over, but which were done by a group you belong to? (Your country or your church, for example).

6. Individually, think of one area where you think that your national or local government is acting wrongly. Write down what is wrong and what you think ought to happen. In pairs, tell each other about this.

Discuss what you might do to change things. Even if you disagree with your partner about the issue, you can make suggestions about how to make his or her point of view heard.

If, between you, you come up with a way to change things – do it!

7. Choose one area of the world where Britain was once colonial ruler. For the next meeting, find out as much as you can about relations between this area and Britain from the British first arriving until the present day. Prepare a presentation to the rest of the group. You may wish to present it as a factual account, or as something more emotive: drama, poetry, a view from the non-British angle. You may wish to focus on just one incident, or take the whole history.

When the group has seen the presentation(s), discuss:
Did Britain rule with justice?
What did Britain gain from its actions?
What did the colonial country gain?
Is there an imbalance? If so, can it be put right now?
Do you feel any responsibility for what went on in the past?
Have you gained any advantages from what happened?

As a group, devise a liturgy, drama or a prayer which expresses what you think and feel about the situation – include the original presentation if you feel it is appropriate.

Is authority from God?

Here we come to what is in many ways the heart of Christian participation in the wider social community. In the 13th chapter of the Epistle to the Romans, Paul makes the challenging statement that the actual governments of the world are fulfilling a commission from God in sustaining the life of society and that the civil authorities are God's ministers. He also says that government is to be obeyed, not only from fear or prudent self interest but 'for conscience's sake', opening the way to a view of responsible political participation which is the pre-condition and life blood of a successfully working democracy. In many ways, many in Europe feel that, while not perfect, Western democracy is certainly one of the best if not the best model of government available. But Romans 13 assumes a reasonably just and benevolent state, one which rewards the good and punishes the evil. What if the state does the opposite?

The writer of the Book of Revelation – a prisoner on the island of Patmos – saw the Roman Empire in a very different light. It was to him 'the Beast' punishing the saints. And in every way, to him, the saints were a sign of contradiction to the powers and principalities of this world. In the end, Paul himself seems to have fallen foul of the authorities and been martyred. Given the injunction 'to obey God rather than man', Christian citizens are therefore thrown back on their own judgement in working out their relationship to the government under which they live. This relationship may involve a positive sharing of responsibility (while maintaining a position of critical independence) or, in situations of injustice or oppression, a call to protest and resistance. Christians in the former German Democratic Republic found in the term 'critical solidarity' a guiding light in the tensions of this relationship.

In Britain and Europe today, the Christian citizen will be a participant in the processes of government at many levels and yet – if sensitive to the demands of the Gospel – will also need to be both able and willing to be called to act in contradiction to the state. In this position of loyal opposition or critical solidarity, the balance is a fine one. The two visions of the state spelt out by Paul and St. John the Divine mean that

Christians can never offer either unquestioning obedience to government nor total resistance.

God's vision of community

What Christians bring is a vision of the world "as it is in heaven" and as could be on earth if God's will were done by all; the Kingdom of God as it is often called in the Gospels. What did Jesus mean when he said that he came to bring the kingdom? Two images capture it and relate it to the needs of this world both material and spiritual. In Luke chapter 4:16-30 we read how Jesus started his ministry in his home town – Nazareth. In doing so he read from the prophet Isaiah:

> "The spirit of the Lord has been given to me,
> for he has anointed me.
> He has sent me to bring good news to the poor,
> to proclaim liberty to the captives
> and to the blind new sight,
> to set the downtrodden free,
> to proclaim the Lord's year of favour."

Any vision of society, any planned community of social, political and economic unity must have these aspects in mind if Christians are to be faithful to the call of Jesus. But alongside this we need to set the vision of the Peace of God which passes all understanding, and that Peace which the world cannot give. The Christian has more than just a social programme to work for. She or he also has to offer that sense of purpose which takes us beyond the here and now and offers us relationship, community and fellowship with God, the God who:

> "though wrapped round with
> the majesty of heaven,
> bends down for the people of earth"

(see page 12)

To be visionary and hopeful today takes a lot of courage. People tend to be very cynical of such hopes and beliefs. In the welfare state, Britain has a model which, for all its blemishes, was a major social **38** breakthrough and one which many Christians would wish to endorse.

Welfare polity for the world

We tend to forget quite what a remarkable achievement the welfare state in the UK is. From the first industrialised, capitalist society of the world, we were able to produce a society in which those who were employed, those who were well off and those who controlled the wealth being created, accepted that it was their duty and responsibility to provide for those who were unemployed; those who were in need; those who were sick or troubled and those who were unable to contribute to the wealth of the nation. This national polity – organising of society – was achieved by the interaction between the Christian social vision, not least of people such as Archbishop William Temple, and through the increased participation of ordinary people in democratic processes. It was, and despite recent attacks remains, a remarkable example of a society deciding to organise itself in such a way as to care for the poor, to tend the sick, to liberate those who are prisoners of forces beyond their control and as a genuine expression of communal responsibility.

As Britain enters Europe more fully, is it too much to hope that Christians and others will continue this development? That in fact a vision of a world polity of social care and concern can be developed? Much of the recent writings of the Roman Catholic Church and of the Pope seem to indicate that the Roman Catholic Church is wanting to assist such a vision to come to fruition. This is based on the Papal Encyclical *Rerum Novarum* (The Modern Situation) of 1891. Since this time there has been a gradual development of Catholic social teaching, with an increased stress on solidarity with the poorest.

If such a vision could be developed in Europe, but not just with a sense of responsibility for the poor and disadvantaged of Europe but also of the world, then government would be living up to the hopes of it expressed by St. Paul in Romans 13. The Social Charter seems to offer something of this, but only with regard to those already within Europe. We need to be looking beyond our own people, to those peoples whose lives we hold in our hands through the power of our banking systems, through our control of world markets, through Europe's involvement in the arms trade and through the use of restrictive practices.

Responsibility as joy and duty

In the Alternative Service Book of the Anglican Church occurs the phrase,

> "It is indeed right, it is our duty and our joy, at all times and in all places to give you thanks and praise"

Perhaps this could be a guiding light for Christian responsibility in this world. Our joy in the love of God helps us to engage in society, and contemplation of the image of God in all peoples should lead us to be responsible to that image in all people. It should be our duty because God first loved us and because Jesus has taught us to see those around us as our brothers and sisters, those for whom we have felt antipathy as our neighbours, and the whole world as being the stage upon which the passion of God is to be worked out.

Many politicians seem to believe that only by offering people more and more material goods can they gain or retain power. Christians, with the sense of both joy and bounden duty, offer another vision of what our responsibilities should be. Our own recent past offers us the model of a society deciding to support all the members of the society and to provide for all in extremis. Is it too much to hope that such a vision could be kept alive and brought to a new intensity through the emerging European and world communities?

8. Are there circumstances when Christians should disobey the government under which they live? How would you define these circumstances?

9. In the specific area of citizenship and responsibility, what do you think it means that human beings are made in the image of God? What aspects of God's nature that we share are important in the area of public life and government?

Source of Life; sixth-century relief from chancel slab, Ravenna.

" TELL ME HOW DOES YOUR WONDERFUL ECONOMY WORK "

WHO PAYS FOR WEALTH?

ECONOMICS AND SOCIETY

Isaiah's vision

At the Malvern Conference 91, the highpoint for many was the Biblical study offered one morning by Professor John Hull, professor of Education at Birmingham University. He took the vision of Isaiah in Isaiah chapter 6 and told it as if he were indeed the prophet. The sheer drama of that story was brought home as John spoke about how paralysed he felt, unable to speak 'for I am a man of unclean lips, and I live among a people of unclean lips'. This, he helped us see, spoke of our condition today, unable to speak because we have become compromised by the society we inhabit and help to form.

When it came to the part of the story concerning the live coal taken with tongs from the fire by the angel, you could feel the whole congregation stir in consternation. John then said 'With this, the angel touched my lips, and the name of the coal was Chernobyl; was Auschwitz; was Glasgow; was Birmingham'. In one dramatic moment, we saw that the pressing social and economic issues of our time were what should burn our lips so that we have to speak up and suffer the distress of bearing an uncomfortable message. You will recall that after Isaiah's lips had been touched by the live coal, he was able to speak again and when God said, 'Whom shall I send? Who will be my messenger?', Isaiah replied 'Here I am, send me.'

We live in a world where those who have, have more, and those who do not have, have even less. We live in a world of social and economic structures about which our feelings are often ambiguous. Many people are frightened by the word 'economics', and overwhelmed by the range of social issues which confront not just our society, but the world at large. In part this comes from our awe of experts and of the extent to which issues have become disguised by language. At another level, it reflects the fact that Christianity has become better at dealing with individuals than with structures. Some of the roots of this lie in chapter 13 of Romans which we looked at in the previous chapter. In part it has come from an assumption that Western societies were, in some ill-defined way, 'Christian', and therefore OK.

At one level, most of us can keep our heads above water, and some are even doing very nicely thank you. We don't really want to rock the boat. Yet we know that within our own society, the gap between the well-off and the poor has increased; the gap between the rich countries and the rest of the world has increased. Yet we are not sure what other system we could really have.

For many, the mixed market economy of private enterprise, state enterprise, social welfare and voluntary concern is about as good a mix as you can get. Some people argue that the market system is the most efficient way to create wealth – and if we do not create wealth we have nothing to share. Inequality is seen as necessary and good, since it fuels the engine of the market system. Inequality in this context is not seen as injustice because no-one actually intends the poor to suffer. According to this view, what is needed is to fine-tune the balance between the market and other factors, so that inequalities are genuinely minimised and opportunities are created for all. Supporters of the market economy claim that this expresses the ideal of freedom. But they tend to ignore fundamental questions about human community.

Others see the mixed economy as favouring those who have at the expense of those who do not have. The collapse of the state run economic systems of Eastern Europe and the USSR has shaken many people's confidence in the possibility of any other system really working. And yet, as the Papal encyclical *Centesimus Annus* says: 'There are many human needs which find no place in the market. It is a strict duty of justice and truth not to allow fundamental human needs to remain unsatisfied.'

A good example of basic human needs not being met by the market economy is unemployment. The market system assumes that a certain number of people will remain unemployed. What happens when factories are forced to shut down because they are no longer competitive? The 'golden handshakes' offered in redundancy payments are hardly sufficient to compensate for the loss of ability to work. Many skilled workers have been trained in specific areas which they cannot easily trade elsewhere. The idea that they can simply 'get on their bike' after twenty years on the job seems callous and unrealistic.

On the other hand, a further question concerns the emphasis we have placed on paid employment. We have created the absurd scenario of the poverty trap where some types of work are so badly paid that the worker may as well be receiving unemployment benefit. Who decides salary scales for particular tasks? Have we forced the powerless to receive less even if our community could not function without them? Do we have to accept that the evolution of high-tech industry means that some unemployment is inevitable? Somehow our sense of self-worth needs to come from who we are rather than whether and how much our particular job is paid. Yet there still remain fundamental questions of justice for those living at the lowest end of the salary scale. The concept of basic income for all, regardless of their paid employment, is an idea which we need to take seriously.

The views from inside and outside

Living inside the house of Western society and economics, many of us find it very hard to imagine what this house – our society – looks like from the outside. Inside the house, we seem to be doing quite well. Things get a bit tight at times and the environment isn't quite what it used to be. To some extent though, we are content to let things go on as they are, hoping to raise a little extra money for a new machine for the hospital or funds for the books at school. We resemble Isaiah before the live coal touched his lips. We are unable to speak the truth because we live amongst the people of unclean lips.

To those outside the house of Western social and economic success – the poor in our own countries and the vast majority of the rest of the world – our society looks very different. To some (indeed, to many) it may look incredibly attractive. Our wealth, our consumer goods, our lifestyle, seem to be a dream, but an achievable dream. The bright lights of this house draw people from all across the world – governments as much as peasants from the countrysides of the third world. But those who enter the house find they are shut off from its comforts. They are forced to live only in the cellar. Governments, attracted by massive loans of money which the West could not use, find that the debt has become a millstone around their necks. Country people who have flocked to the cities of both the industrialised nations and the emerging industrialised nations, find themselves living in greater poverty than they did in the countryside.

Some of them protest. Some of those within the house itself hear this protest and join in. But for many, the great question is, what other way could things be run? It is no part of Christian faith to promote chaos, but rather to seek some way of ordering the ways of the world that respects the image of God in all.

In the Trinity Prayer in chapter one, Jesus is described as the 'Troubler of the powerful' while the Holy Spirit is described as the 'Inspirer and Disturber'. These ideas are found also in Mary's song of praise to God, the Magnificat (Luke 1:46-55), and were emphasised in John Hull's retelling of Isaiah. We are called to ask the questions, to speak and to act with integrity based upon the vision of God continually sustaining all creation and all people. This means that we have an uncomfortable role to play. Our responsibility is to work with economists, sociologists and politicians to probe deeply into the way our society is run and into the way it uses its resources. We must avoid settling for the easy and undemanding – the untroubling.

Economics and Society

Turn to questions
on next page

1. (For private meditation and prayer) –
Read Isaiah 6:1-8. Try to read it as though the prophet were yourself, now. For example:
'In the year that . . .' What public events mark this year for you?
'I am lost, for . . .' What things in yourself would make you ashamed to meet God?
'And I live among a people . . .' What things in our society cut us off from God?
'With this it touched my mouth . . .' Allow yourself to be hurt by some of the pain God feels.
Continue to the end of the passage in this way.

2. In the text above, Western society and economy was described in terms of a house whose lights draw people from all over the world. Where do you feel that you live in the house? (For example, the servant's quarters, the best living-room, etc.) How much do you know about the lives of those in other parts of the house, or outside it?

3. In pairs, role-play a conversation between people living in different relationships to Western economies. Tell each other about your lives, and what Western society looks like to you.

4. People often judge their own or other people's value by the job they do and how much they are paid for it. Would this be so even if everyone had enough to live on without working? Would it still be important for people to work? How much does your sense of your own worth come from having, or not having, a job? What else gives you a sense of worth?

5. Read 1 Corinthians 12:12-26. In what ways are people dependent on each other? Does this idea extend to your working and earning as well as to your church life?

The factory and the first aid post

A story might help. Once upon a time, there was a woman walking
past a factory. As she passed the gates, a worker came stumbling out,

his hand bleeding from a cut received from one of the machines. The woman, moved by pity, bandaged his hand. While she was doing this another person came out, also injured. Soon the woman found that she was needed every day at the factory gate to treat those who were injured. She appealed to her friends, her church and the local community for volunteers to assist her and soon a regular group was functioning there running a first aid post with a small hut to keep the rain off and supplies provided by a support group. The next step was for the support group to raise enough money to build a clinic and trained medical staff were taken on. The factory workers were getting the best treatment possible and funds came flowing in from church bazaars, school performances and such like. Within a couple of years, a small hospital had been built, with a donation from the factory owners.

Then one day, the woman who had started all this stopped working in the hospital and looked at the rows of injured workers. She looked at the trained medical staff and she looked at the factory. She suddenly realised that it was no good tending the wounded workers. What was needed was to change the way the factory worked so that workers were not being exposed to such risks of injury. So she entered the factory to challenge the way things were done.

This story is only a story, but it raises certain key issues. It is often easier to treat the symptoms than to tackle the cause. Christians have a long and honourable history of dealing with the symptoms, but less of a history of tackling the causes. This is because, especially in Protestant Europe, we have tended to concentrate on the needs and redemption of the individual rather than on the problems inherent in the structures. A real challenge to the Churches to day is whether we can develop an adequate theology and practice of *structural redemption*. Let us look at an example.

Faith in the City

In Britain, we already have an example of the Church playing a disturbing and caring role in an area of immense social and economic concern: the inner cities. In 1985 the Church of England issued the **49**

Report of the Archbishop of Canterbury's Commission on Urban Priority Areas, known as *Faith in the City*. This report called for the Church and the Nation to take account of the:

> "growing number of people [who] are excluded by poverty or powerlessness from sharing in the common life of our nation. A substantial minority – perhaps as many as one person in four or five across the nation, and a much higher proportion in the Urban Priority Areas – are forced to live on the margins of poverty or below the threshold of an acceptable standard of living."

(Page 359)

The response of the Government was to try and dismiss the report as a piece of left-wing, Marxist social tinkering. But the report set out clearly both the limits and the extents of what it saw as being the consequences of the report and its findings.

> "The Church cannot supplant the market or the state. It can, as we recommend, mobilize its own resources in a way that accords high priority to the poor. It must by example and its exertions proclaim the ethic of altruism against egotism, of community against self-seeking, and of charity against greed."

(Page 359)

The Church of England began a process which was remarkably similar to that of entering the gates of the factory rather than staying in the clinic or hospital at the gates. It began to look at its own distribution of wealth, which has always favoured the middle-class suburbs. It began to organise quotas which would provide a major financial fund for use in the inner cities. It linked parishes from the affluent parts of its community with parishes in the inner city. Many painful discoveries were made by both sides as parishes in for instance, leafy Cambridge were linked to parishes in inner city Manchester. The 'poor' were no longer the unknown. They were found to be members of the same Church.

Since 1985 the Church Urban Fund has been engaged in a variety of projects across the country. Some fall into the old first aid category. But some are attempting to change reality in small but powerful ways.

The issue of powerlessness and control over one's own life has emerged time and again. Here is just one example.

Congregations Organised for a Greater Bristol – COGB for short – aims at giving ordinary people the power to change their lives for the better. It is a coalition of twenty-seven member organisations, most of which are Christian. In its first few months, COGB can claim considerable success through public actions about issues its strategy team has identified as being of wide public concern.

– A late night delegation around an industrial estate resulted in a local factory spending £2,000 to eliminate processing noises that kept families awake at night.
– The group has raised the possibility of action to improve safety for children crossing a busy road to get to school. The traffic lights allow them seven seconds to get across, but are too old to be adjusted. COGB has brought the council and developers together publicly to try and solve the problem.
– COGB has challenged the biggest local building society, the Bristol and West, to give £600,000 a year, one per cent of its pre-tax profits, to help the homeless. After months of stonewalling and a silent vigil by COGB members outside its annual meeting, the association has agreed to review its policy.

These actions help to improve the quality of life but they are seen as secondary to the main aims of COGB. One of the organisers says, "It is about enabling people to see that they are not powerless and to release the talents of potential leaders from the community. We acknowledge where power is and we are anxious about unaccountable power."

Turn to questions on next page

6. When the woman entered the factory to challenge the way it worked, what do you think happened to her? Write a story or make a play showing what opposition she met, how she dealt with it, who helped her, etc.

7. Mary sang the Magnificat when she knew she was bearing the Saviour of the world. Reflect on her words, especially Luke 1:51-53, in the light of this.

8. In what way is Britain or Europe like the factory that is harming others? Who can help us see what our 'factory' is doing to others? (for example, partners in mission, television programmes such as 'World in Action', etc.) How can we hear those voices in our schools, churches, or workplace?

The inevitable march of consumerism?

In the eighties, consumerism was elevated to new levels of veneration by many within Western Europe. The age of the conspicuous consumer left many Christians feeling uncomfortable, but few wishing to be like the gloomy guests at a birthday party and actually protest.

Gradually, some began to realise that there were two big problems with such consumerism. Firstly, it left more and more people struggling at the bottom of the pile, feeling worthless because they did not have a video, new car and hi-fi. Secondly, the costs to the natural environment were terrible. By the late eighties, many consumers had developed a concern for ecology. But this still left untouched the basic issue of whether, even with recycling, the planet can afford the relative luxury of the Western European lifestyle.

Then Eastern Europe entered the scene. Here were millions of people (250 million) suddenly freed from the shackles of state control. The message went out that here was the next great new market. The vision which suddenly filled many people's minds was of a rapid inclusion of these millions in the lifestyle of Western Europe. Cherished values in the former ordering of Eastern Europe in areas such as preventative medicine, affordable housing and employment, were lost almost overnight. Instead, the great new social and economic hope became the free market, free enterprise and consumerism.

The planet cannot support 250 million extra consumers in the life-style to which we in the West of Europe and in North America, have become accustomed. Yet this is what the peoples of Eastern Europe have been led to expect. It is as though we were standing at the gate, not bandaging the wounds, but selling elaborately flavoured icecreams.

A fundamental social and economic question has to be asked. Is the assumed consumer-driven society which is being planned or projected for Eastern Europe and for so many other parts of the world either desirable or achievable? If it is, then we need to know how this is going to be sustained and how those who fail in such a competitive world are to be cared for; where the natural resources are to come from to fuel, feed and provide goods for such a vast market. If the answer is no, then we have to face the fact that our present lifestyle is almost certainly unsustainable.

Economics and Society

---

9. In the Trinity Prayer, Jesus is described as 'Troubler', the Holy Spirit as 'Disturber'. What should the people of God be?

10. When East Germans first went through the Berlin Wall and saw West German life at first hand, some of them came back saying, 'Yes, it's very attractive, but it's not what we want for our country.' Within a year, the two countries had voted to become one, and the East German system was completely taken over by the West German.
   a) Why do you think this happened?
   b) What have the people of East Germany gained?
   c) What have they lost?

Faith in the world?

The stories from *Faith in the City* are local ones, UK examples. But what of the injustices and problems faced by the wider world community? For many peoples of the world, it is a simple matter of lack of control over their own lives and over their own wealth and skills. This is often compounded by state systems which have squandered the

53

wealth of the country and the loans/aid grants given to it on ostentatious lifestyles, armaments and other trappings of power, which have offered little to their people.

Some Christians took refuge in the text from Romans quoted in chapter 2. Others cut off and sought to engage in first aid work. For some Christians, the only answer is to be involved in armed revolution against such unjust systems. But experience, painfully learned since the Second World War shows that little ever changes and that the human and social costs of such upheavals are often even worse than the effects of the unjust system.

But amongst many of the Christian aid agencies new ideas have started to emerge. The idea of helping people to bypass existing economic structures and to create their own economic or social movement. An example of this is the one grain of rice movement. It began in India, where a church group was concerned about the poverty of the women, their lack of control over land or any other means to feed their families, and the degradation of the land itself, which was often over-farmed and left eroded and useless. The women themselves got together and promised each other that, no matter how hungry they were, each day each of them would put aside one grain of rice. At the end of the week they pooled their rice, and soon had a few cupfuls which could be sold. They saved this money until they had enough to buy the lease on a small piece of land which had become unproductive and left derelict. Together the women worked on this land, planting trees, terracing against erosion, and gradually restoring its fertility. When they began to grow crops on it, they had gained some control over their own lives. This idea has now spread to many parts of India and Pakistan, and some places in Africa.

11. The Trinity Prayer describes Jesus as the troubler of the powerful, and the Holy Spirit as the disturber. In some circumstances, might this mean that Christians are called to support revolution against unjust systems?

12. Read Matthew 20:20-28, and discuss:
a) What are your ambitions for your children?
b) What are or were your parents' ambitions for you?
c) How does this affect your attitude to wealth and power?

13. Find out about self-help schemes in other parts of the world. Are there ways in which you can support these efforts without making people dependent?

14. In ancient Jewish law, as set out in the Old Testament, the poor had certain rights, such as that of gleaning the grain that was left in the fields, and the producers had certain duties towards them, such as leaving some corn unharvested. What equivalents might be possible in our society to allow people to help themselves?

15. Draw up a set of principles on which you think that wealth distribution should be based. For example, should it be based on people's needs or on their contribution to society? How would you measure either of these? What problems arise in trying to draw up these principles?

Economics and Society

Who is in control?

The World Bank is a vast international loan scheme, established after the Second World War to direct development in areas of the world where poverty and hunger threatened. Its basic goals were and are honourable. Its results have largely been disastrous. It has poured money into regimes and projects which no one wanted. It has come to cultures with a grand plan which took no account of the hopes and aspirations of the local people nor of their wisdom and insights. The results have been expensive schemes which didn't just fail; they caused massive ecological disasters and economic hardship.

In the early 1980s, aid agencies and environmental groups targeted the World Bank, through a mixture of pressure on member countries and lobbying generally. In 1985, the World Bank had a handful of environmentalists on its staff. Now it has over a thousand, and no project can be approved without a thorough environmental impact assessment. The Bank still funds bad projects; there are still projects which it is overseeing which are inappropriate; but increasingly the Bank is trying to listen to the voices of those it formerly ignored, and is trying to act in accordance with the genuine long-term interests of the peoples and the environment of given areas. Here is a massive economic organisation which has begun to change. As Christians, we are able to believe that individuals can be converted and redeemed from the foolishness or evil of their past. Yet we seem to be very hesitant in hoping for and striving after the same sort of repentance or conversion of structures. In this, we may well have been failing the world.

A second example is a more vexed one, but a challenging one. The European Community's Social Charter. Many have feared that the growth of a politically and economically more integrated Europe will mean the survival of the fittest. The Social Charter seems to offer at least some signs that such a massive structure can, should and could undertake to incorporate social and economic justice into its very foundations. The Social Charter is capable of being seen in a number of ways. One is that it is the beginnings of a social welfare polity for Europe, which harks back to the World polity mentioned at the end of chapter 2. As such, there are some in the entrepreneurial world who fear this as a burden on the free play of market forces. This is probably exactly what it should be, for the strength of the European systems is their mixture of social and private market forces.

Others see the Charter as clearing the ground for the better and most efficient use of workers and of social structures for wealth creation. The direction in which the Social Charter will go and the implications which it could have are still in the melting pot. As such, the involvement of Christians in discussing and constructing the Social Charter is very important. Here is a document which could begin to help us face up to some of the inequalities and social hardships caused by our economic systems. Christians should engage with this, and thus have a role in saying who is in charge and why.

The issue of needs and wants brings us back to the question of values. What is it that we really value in our society? What common concerns unite us even when we express these concerns differently? On any list, the following are likely to appear: decent housing; education; security; health provision; a role for all, in fulltime work or not; equal opportunities for access to higher education or training. It is important for any society, but especially for Christians, to sort out the difference between needs and wants. For example, the ability to travel freely and easily could be described as a need. But the means to that end is of crucial importance. By saying that the ability to travel is a need, we are not therefore saying everyone should have cars. Far from it, it may be more important for everyone to have access to good public transport, since cars inflict so much damage on the environment. Our need may be for travel: the want is for my car.

Much of what we use for travel, food, clothing, heating and so forth is destructive of the environment. It uses up resources which cannot be replaced. This will be explored more fully in the next two chapters, but let us just pose one question. In the normal way of estimating the wealth of a country, we talk about the Gross National Product (GNP). This measures what a country produces in the way of manufactured goods, food, raw resources etc. What is never taken into account is what it costs to produce these things. Thus, the industrialised countries are usually shown as having a high GNP, and this is taken as an indicator of how successful they are. Yet to do this they are often stripping their environment and the environment of other countries of irreplacable raw materials such as coal, oil or minerals. They are over-using resources which are becoming rapidly depleted with no sign of any attempt to restock – hardwood forests; fish stocks; soil and even clean water systems.

We must try to find better ways of measuring the 'success' of a nation or an economy: ways which measure the stress that it places on the environment by its use of raw materials and energy, and such human factors as the quality of the health and education of its people, and whether production is related to human needs or to consumer wants. We need to use new indicators of what wealth and wealth creation really mean.

16. Try using the model of needs and wants on other issues (for example, recreation and holidays) and see what sort of picture begins to emerge of where our society should be putting its energies and skills.

17. Allow yourselves to be idealistic, and if necessary unrealistic. Spend some time individually on a list which begins:
'I want a Britain where . . . ', in which you picture a just society.

If you change 'Britain' to 'Europe' or 'world', do you have to add anything to your list?
Make your lists as specific as you can, for that is where you will discover differences with the rest of the group. Discuss your differences and try to draw up a common list. This may not be possible, and you may wish to put in several 'minority reports'.

Then discuss what might be done to bring this about:
a) by you individually
b) by your government
c) by European governments acting together.
Write to your MP or MEP with some of your ideas.

Ultimately, social and economic theories and systems claim to be valid because they meet the needs of people. They are ultimately only tools of a set of values. What we as Christians need to do, in any society, is to look very closely at whether social and economic policies are designed to meet the needs of the people and of God's creation, or whether they have become gods in their own right, setting themselves above the common good and meeting only the needs and frequently the wants of the powerful. If so, then Christians need to listen more carefully to the words of the Magnificat; need to look for the places where the first aid post is no longer relevant and to seek to name the live coal which is being offered to them – painful as this may be.

MASTERS
OF THE UNIVERSE?

SCIENCE AND TECHNOLOGY

Dr.Jekyll or Mr.Hyde?

In popular science fiction, or 'James Bond' thrillers, the scientist is usually shown in one of two ways. There is the good scientist who is using his or her skills to try and solve a major problem; searching after knowledge which may at first seem unrelated to real needs but is shown to be the key to solving the mystery. Such scientists are dedicated to the search for knowledge. They are implacably opposed to strong men, dictators, mad rulers and the like who wish to use the scientists' knowledge for personal power or national control. Such scientists would never dream of selling out to vested interests – they are the pure priests of knowledge.

The second image is that of the mad scientist. The power-crazed scientist who is in league with the forces of evil. These scientists are searching for knowledge in order to serve a vile end – world control or the like. They are so obsessed with their quest for knowledge and/or power that they will willingly sacrifice anything and anyone who gets in their way. Their skills are for sale to the highest bidder, and they are willing to be involved in the use of their knowledge in ways which threaten the wellbeing of many.

Both of these images are of course extremes. Yet they reflect a perception of science in our culture which is very ambiguous. Is science good or bad? Are individual scientists good or bad?

Towards the end of the last century and into the early years of this century, great hopes for a new world order were placed on the shoulders of science. It was believed that science could answer all our problems; that by scientific means we could engineer human life and behaviour, so that everyone could be made content. Science was seen as a pure form of knowledge, unmarred by religious, sectarian or ideological values: a value-free system which could really help us to understand and, by understanding, to control the world and ourselves.

Then came the World Wars, when science provided the means for biological warfare, for greater and more terrible weapons; when scientists worked in the concentration camps carrying out destructive experiments on living human beings. The result was the beginning of a deep suspicion of science. The suspicion has continued to this day and has provoked something of a crisis of confidence for scientists and for science: a crisis, ironically, not dissimilar to that which Christianity has undergone (see chapter one).

The Crisis of Confidence

The Archbishop of York, himself a scientist, has spoken of the nature of this crisis of confidence in science. He described it, when speaking at the opening of the Malvern Conference 91, as a collapse in confidence, which was forcing scientists re-evaluate scientific style. He spoke of the need to bring *humanness* back into science, to be balanced alongside analysis. He called for the wider adoption of a 'wholistic' approach in science; for a greater concern not just with the facts, but also with the context of scientific knowledge. The exact sciences have made the disastrous mistake of excluding all that is personal and spiritual, leaving them unable to respond to the great moral and ethical challenges which confront us. In other words we must bring values and beliefs back into the heart of science and recognise that, whether we like it or not, science is used for specific ends, and therefore must have a vision of the wholeness and meaning of life within which to find its place and role.

Science
and
Technology

The West has long cherished the belief that science could be value-free. The Archbishop of York was saying that science has always been an outworking of the human culture from which it comes, even when it is exploring the unknown. Not only do individual scientists have their own personal beliefs, but the kind of questions scientists ask, the very language in which they express the answers and the priorities expressed in funding, all express the beliefs of a particular culture. We need to ask:
What values does science spring from?
What values should science express?
Who is science currently serving?

1. Take films or books that you have seen in the last few years. What is the image of the scientist that comes across?

2. When you were younger, did you ever hope or plan to be a scientist? Why? What was your image of a scientist? Has it changed now?

3. Many groups appeal for money for scientific research, especially for medical problems. What motives do they appeal to? What claims do they make? Why do they think that 'science' is a good selling-point? Does it make you want to give money?

4. Try the same exercise on advertisements for 'scientifically proven' or 'environmentally safe' products.

Science and the role of technology

In the West, we are used to talking about science and technology as related but separate. Many would hold that it is possible to undertake pure scientific research, with no concern for any application. The applications are seen as technology. Indeed, most of our scientific training assumes this to be the norm. In other parts of the world, this division is seen as a falsehood, willingly followed by the West because it exonerates its scientists from the consequences of their research. In places such as the Philippines, the idea of science and technology being separate is seen as ridiculous. Poor countries cannot afford the luxury of the pure search after knowledge. They have massive technological problems – how to feed their people, how to harness nature without destroying it, how to develop appropriate technology for the village or small community. For them, science has to be the handmaiden of technology, seeking to meet the basic needs of the people. In such societies, it is much clearer what role science should play in serving the wider needs of the society.

But in our society, we seem to have no clear picture or sense of direction for science. We believe that science is the quest for knowledge. It may or may not give rise to some application, but that is of secondary importance to the knowledge itself. On closer scrutiny this fine old academic vision doesn't stand up. The majority of scientists employed in Europe are engaged in work related to the armaments trade. Of the remainder, many are employed by commercial companies, working to develop or improve consumer goods and services. To get a grant to do research even in the universities means finding a commercial sponsor, or else an 'angle' for selling the idea to the Government. Thus while we might like to believe in pure science, we would be very hard pressed to find any substantial evidence to show that science in Europe is not merely driven by technology, or by pressure from consumers and arms manufacturers. The days of the scientist just working for the love of knowledge seem to be numbered. These days the scientist is being tempted to sell his or her skills to the highest bidder, almost regardless of the use to which the buyer will put such knowledge.

In order to illustrate this, let's look at two stereotypes of scientists. We offer these as deliberate contrasts so that issues can be put into high relief.

For love of God or mammon?

Much of the basic scientific work of the early 19th century was undertaken by amateurs. These amateurs were the leisured classes who could afford to give time to study and research. High in numbers amongst these early scientists were country clergy. To this day, foundation papers or studies on topics as diverse as plant types; classification of species or the study of archaeology owe their origins to clergymen. Take a well known example, the Rev. Keble-Martin. A country vicar all his life, he compiled and illustrated the standard flora of the United Kingdom. His beautifully illustrated book is a basic text for botanists, and his careful notes have not been surpassed in many areas of observations about certain species.

He undertook such studies out of a love of knowledge and a belief that God was the creator of all, and thus that all was worthy of study and reflection. His was a labour of love as is witnessed by his exquisite paintings.

Consider now the image of the average research scientist at work in a major company. His or her work is waged, and is dependent upon the interests of the company. It is goal-orientated and the goal is to increase knowledge about some product which can be marketed, or to find some sort of improvement to an existing product which will ensure that the company keeps its competitive edge in the market place.

Now, at one level, the company's scientists are not a problem. The usefulness of their research is judged, in part, by us the consumers. But much of what we want is shaped by advertising and peer-group pressure; by self-interest and perhaps greed. Is this really how we want science to be controlled? It could, however, work the other way. If consumers demand a better environment and a higher level of environmental concern from industry, then the company has to take note. Take, for example, the washing powder box. In the recent past, the manufacturers produced bigger and bigger boxes with more and more powder and for a 'brighter' wash. Now the emphasis is against big and in favour of small. We don't want big cardboard boxes which cannot be recycled. Not only do we want smaller boxes, but we are not so hung up on 'whiter than white', because we know that this means lots of 'unfriendly' chemicals. Thus the companies have discovered, through their research scientists, how to make a more concentrated powder which uses smaller boxes and which has less impact on the environment.

We find other concrete examples of the way science is shaped by consumer demand in the agro-sciences. Most of the research effort in the UK is directed towards crop plants which can be grown in this country. Research into increasing the performance of subsistence crops grown in the Third World is not given priority, because for us there is no immediate profit. In terms of planning and direction of research, short-term gain wins over the long-term benefit of helping the poor feed themselves, so once again those in developing countries are forced to rely on surplus grain produced by the affluent West.

The issues which arise from all this are really rather basic ones. Who is in control of our scientific knowledge, and why? Who shapes the use of scientific knowledge, and why? Whose values are inspiring scientific work today – and are they the ones which really offer a hope and future for the world?

When the Gulf War was about to start, people were understandably frightened of the possible use of biological weapons, of the possibilities of nuclear warheads or of the nuclear radiation likely to come from bombed Iraqi nuclear power plants. Yet all these weapons and power plants are the products of our own scientists and scientific culture. We had sold raw materials and components to Iraq ourselves. With so much of our nation's wealth, worker time and scientists involved in armaments, we have to be able to sell them to someone in order to keep the money rolling in. Yet this is producing exactly the kind of unstable world which we all fear. Something has gone wrong in our understanding of both the role of science and the application of it through technology and its relationship to industry.

---

5. In what ways has science improved your life?

6. "He undertook such studies out of a love of knowledge and a belief that God was the creator of all, and thus that all was worthy of study and reflection. His was a labour of love, as is witnessed by his exquisite paintings." (see p.65)
   If this was what guided science today, what major differences would you expect to see in:
   a) who would fund science?
   b) what research would be undertaken?
   c) where the results of research would be applied?.

7. Think of a possible scientific project that might need to apply for funds. Split the group into two. Each is to draw up an application for funds for this project:
   – one assuming that the values outlined in the previous question are dominant
   – the other applying to a commercial concern like those which fund most research today.
   Compare your two applications.

8. How much power do you have, as a consumer, to affect the way science is applied to your everyday life? Have you ever tried to use this power?

**Science
and
Technology**

Finding Wisdom

In our Trinity Prayer, the Holy Spirit is described as 'Midwife of change, Revealer of hidden truth.' The search for knowledge and the use of it to bring about change is a natural part of being human. This returns us to the theme of humanity as being creative because made in the image of a creative God. The search for a greater understanding of the workings of God is natural for Christians. Foremost amongst the early pioneers of what we see as 'modern' science, were many Franciscans. As wandering friars, taught by St. Francis to observe God's creation, the Franciscans studied and recorded what they actually saw on their travels, unlike the monks who stayed in their monasteries and simply read about nature. For the early Franciscans, to observe nature and to note its diversity was to celebrate God. In today's science, the passive observation of nature has now been largely superseded by the manipulation of nature.

It is important to understand that the Bible encourages the exploration of God's world, but within an overall moral, ethical and spiritual context of love. Because it is not included as part of the text of most Protestant editions of the Bible, the Book of Wisdom from the Jewish Bible (always contained within the Roman Catholic translations of the Bible) is not as well known as it should be. The following text comes from Wisdom 7:7 -8; and selections from chapter 7:7 – chapter 8:1.

"And so I prayed, and understanding was given me;
I entreated, and the spirit of Wisdom came to me.
I esteemed her more than sceptres and thrones;
compared with her, I held riches as nothing . . .

May God grant me to speak as he would wish
and express thoughts worthy of his gifts,
since he is the guide of Wisdom,
since he directs the sages.
We are indeed in his hand, we ourselves and our words,
with all our understanding too, and our technical knowledge.
It was he who gave me true knowledge of all that is,
who taught me the structure of the world and the properties of the
elements,

the beginning, end and middle of times,
the alternation of the solstices and the succession of the seasons,
the revolution of the year and the positions of the stars,
the nature of animals and the instincts of wild beasts,
the powers of the spirits and the mental processes of humans,
the varieties of plants and the medicinal properties of their roots.
All that is hidden, all that is plain, I have come to know,
instructed by Wisdom who designed them all . . .

She is the breath of the power of God,
pure emanation of the glory of the Almighty . . .

Although alone, she can do all;
herself unchanging, she makes all things new . . .

She deploys her strength from one end of the earth to the other,
ordering all things for good."

(Jerusalem Bible)

It is sad that this text and others like it within the book of Wisdom are not better known. It was not for nothing that one of the greatest churches of Christianity, the marvellous basilica in the heart of Constantinople was called Hagia Sophia – Holy Wisdom. By not knowing texts such as this, many Christians have felt a certain uncertainty about science. Was it probing where it ought not to go? Was it in some way committing again the sin of eating the fruit of forbidden knowledge? It is ironic that Christianity, which helped create the social and intellectual climate for the surge of scientific exploration which occurred from the late medieval period onwards, has also had a very hesitant relationship with science. Science, pursued in the context of faith described above, should be welcomed by Christians.

This brings us to a crunch point. Where many Christians have parted company with science has been in its attempts to claim that it is not subject to any moral or ethical constraints, because it is engaged in 'pure research'. Is there really is a sustainable divide between science and technology; between knowledge and the use of knowledge?

9. Some people see science as in some way replacing God. From the passage from Wisdom quoted above, what do you think is God's relationship to scientific knowledge, and to the human search for knowledge?

10. Many Christians are inspired with a sense of wonder and thanksgiving to God by meditating on natural objects. Think of a man-made, technical object, which gives you pleasure or a sense of wonder at its ingenuity, whether or not you understand how it works – for example the telephone (which was invented because Alexander Graham Bell wanted news of his sick mother, and was worried by the delay in receiving letters).
Meditate on your chosen object and give thanks to God for it.

Dismembering the world

Another concern voiced by the Archbishop of York is the need to regain a sense of the whole. Our knowledge has become so great that many of us are now deeply engrossed in the detailed study of a tiny part of the whole. This is the fruit of the reductionist method. The whole is reduced down to discernible parts, which are then studied in isolation from each other. In this process the links or inter-relationships between the different parts are lost, overlooked or dismissed. The wholistic vision of knowledge expressed in the book of Wisdom means that each part must be seen as a part of the whole. And the whole is seen as being under God.

The loss of the wholistic vision has reduced our understanding of how things fit and relate together. This is how biological weapons came to be developed. At one level, there is a fascinating scientific venture to be undertaken: that of identifying and isolating the most destructive processes within a biological entity. The further step of controlling these processes within a laboratory is yet another scientific and technological challenge. By this time we are a long way away from the original plant or organism. It is but one further step to develop the isolated and extracted poison for warfare. In a sense the scientists involved in the research are practising pure science. But we are all at risk if they forget to look at both the context within which they work, at who pays the bills and why, and at the end product of their work. Reductionism can reduce our moral and ethical horizons to an alarming degree.

A more wholistic approach, an approach which would put such research into a wider human, social, economic and environmental context, would also affect scientific method itself. The reductionist method is to proceed step by step. Yet most major breakthroughs have come by people following their instincts, their intuition. A failure to recognise the role of the intuition in science has meant a narrowing of our concept of scientific method. Some would see in this a case of science becoming too 'masculine' in its vision of reality by excluding the more 'feminine' aspect of intuition. An example might help to illustrate what is meant.

Intuition and the manual

Three Mile Island is the name of a place in the United States of America where a nuclear power plant nearly melted down and exploded. On the night when this happened, three men were on duty. As the lights began to flash in a sequence previously unseen, the three men reacted in different ways. One man, using intuition, immediately deduced what had happened and suggested to his colleagues what was happening. They refused to accept the suggestion, dismissing it as ridiculous. The evidence for such a deduction was not yet before their eyes. Instead they grabbed the two-inch thick manual and tried to work out what the flashing lights meant. Needless to say no sooner had they decoded one set of signals than the plant moved a step closer to disaster and began to send a new set of signals. Soon they were unable to keep up at all. At this point they turned to their colleague and asked him what he had said right at the beginning. Only then did they realise he had been right and then they were able to take preventive action which saved the power plant from exploding and destroying vast stretches of the state.

In the enquiry afterwards, the intuition of the one man was praised. The official commission recognised that it was this and this alone which had stopped the power plant melting down. The net result was that the manual grew in size from two inches to three!

In looking for the development of a more wholistic outlook in science, the role of intuition needs to be explored further, and steps taken away from the reductionist attitude.

---

11. When you are trying to make decisions, what role does intuition play, and what role does analysis play (For example, do you make lists?) Might you benefit from giving either of these more attention?

12. Take a recent detective story that you have read or seen on television. Discuss the balance between concentrating on details, and intuition about the whole pattern, in solving the mystery.

13. Do you think that science is now regaining a right balance between reductionism and a more wholistic view? Can you give some examples that you agree on within the group?

Going too far

There is however, one other major area of concern about science. Should there be boundaries placed around science, and in particular around the range and depth of its enquiries?

Many people are worried by the areas into which science is now going, and the uses which are or could be made of the knowledge thus gained. An area of major concern, not least to those of us who profess faith in God the creator, is genetic engineering – what is now often called bio-technology. Should there be limits placed on science's ability to work in these areas?

As a species we have been engaged in bio-technology for thousands of years. For instance, we have made the cow produce milk all year round – this is bio-technology. We have bred sheep so that they produce as much wool as possible. This too is biotechnology. We have developed special strands of wheat or barley which give the maximum yield and which do not shed their seeds. So there is nothing new in biotechnology. What is new is the use to which we are now putting it. For instance, can we 'own' a new species or sub-species? A new strand of mouse has been created in the laboratory. It has been designed in order to give maximum results for laboratory experimentation. The inventors of this strand of mouse have successfully applied to patent the mouse in order to reap the fullest financial benefit from their research.

Such a development raised profound moral and spiritual issues. By what right does a company patent a life form? If we allow mice to be patented, what is to stop us moving on to more and more complex creatures until, like Dr Frankenstein, we arrive at new forms of human beings?

The question of the proper limits to scientific enquiry and the use of scientific information is one which splits the Church down the middle. Some feel that science should have clear boundaries placed around it. 'Do not eat of this fruit' might be one way of putting it. Others, only too well aware that that which is forbidden becomes all the more attractive, is indulged in in secret and thus becomes even harder to control, are against any such forced controls. They hope for self-regulation.

The issue is a vexed one. There are developments now which literally put the world at risk. Nuclear weapons, biological weapons, our tampering with the basic structures of so many ecosystems, the polluting of the waters, the using up of natural resources – all these are the results of scientific experimentation and their implementation through technology. Thus it seems a bit arbitrary to pick on something like bio-technology as a major cause for concern. Perhaps we should understand its role as being a visible sign of a deeper fear and anxiety about the role of science and technology in our society.

The value of animal life

The issue of the goals and values of science is hotly debated within the scientific community itself. Take the issue of animals used in experimentation. In most cases, the use of live animals is unnecessary. There are perfectly good alternative methods which can be used to test for reaction to many substances. To use animals in unnecessary and painful ways is a decision which owes more to a concept of our role as master over nature than to any scientific view. We have never developed a clear enough understanding of the rights or nature of other living creatures. The theological debate about whether animals have rational souls is now continued in the debate about whether they have rights. The issue remains the same. If we grant that animals have a rational soul or rights to be protected against pain, we would find it very hard to justify carrying out on them many sorts of experiments.

However, in our culture most people would probably agree that some use of other life-forms (rabbits, frogs etc.) may be necessary in order that significant medical advances can be made. The question is who decides what is likely to be a significant medical advance and should there be any limit to the amount of life taken or pain inflicted in making this advance?

In other cultures, where animals are seen as being filled with the same rational 'soul' or divine spark as humans, animal experimentation is virtually unheard of. In recent years, Buddhist and Hindu students have won the right to work on models intead of real frogs or rabbits in biology lessons at school. They are asking us to place a limit upon the use of living creatures for the passing on of general knowledge. The success of the Body Shop, with its policy of not testing products on live animals or using animal products in its cosmetics, has shown how out of line with current thinking much of the scientific community really is. It will change, but the resistance to change is because science is wedded to an earlier and more convenient model of the place of animals in the world order. One which, as we shall see in the next chapter, has led us to create many of the ecological problems we have today, and which raises profound theological questions, also explored in Chapter 5.

Science will always reflect values, but whose values and to what end? In the USSR, psychiatry is just beginning to recover from being used for social and political ends greatly at odds with its professed aims. The abuse of psychiatric hospitals and of the techniques of psychiatry within the Soviet system is rightly deplored. Here was a science being used to destroy free will, to make people conform or to change them into what the state wanted. Science was used to serve goals which we find terrible, but is this worse than science being used to create even more terrible weapons of mass destruction? A case perhaps of Jesus's warning about seeing the speck in the other person's eye without seeing the beam in our own.

---

14. Do you think that Christians should oppose the use of animals in school experiments?

15. Imagine that the European Community has set up a body to provide guidelines for the direction of science and scientific research. Draw up a document that you would send to this body, describing what the guidelines should be.

16. What do you think are the main social problems that science should be concentrating on? Choose one and work out:
a) Who would you try to influence to make this a priority?
b) How would you influence them?

Science and technology are a part, and only a part, of the wider societies within which they function. Gone are the days when utopian writers of the early 20th century dreamed of a world run by science, modifying our behaviour through drugs which would ensure we were always happy and content, or organising society so that there were suitable grades of humans created for the different roles in life. Aldous Huxley's *Brave New World* helped put paid to that. Yet we still seem to be left with certain hangovers of that age. Pure science is still spoken of as if it existed outside the values, needs and wants of a given society. The issue for Christians is to have a vision of that wider society, its place within the world of humanity and within the overall world of God's creation, by which the role which science can play, and its priorities for research, can be properly judged and chosen.

TRAVERSING THE RAIN FOREST ISN'T THE EXPERIENCE
IT USED TO BE....

NEW HEAVEN, NEW EARTH

THE ENVIRONMENT

Consumers of Eden

"One foot in Eden still, I stand
And look across the other land.
The world's great day is growing late . . ."

With these words of Edwin Muir the Archbishop of Canterbury, Dr.
George Carey, issued a warning to those who would hear. In his ser-
mon in the opening worship at the Malvern Conference 91 he said:

"It is because of the conspicuous consumption of the West that
the planet is faced with diminishing non-renewable resources and
increased world pollution."

Turning to the Christian tradition, the Archbishop declared that

"We seek . . . to work with the natural creation that we may
stand again to overlook the Eden which has been left far behind."

Recent papal encyclicals such as *Solicitudo Res Socialis* (1988) and
Centesimus Annus (1991), also link environmental problems with
consumerism. The 1990 papal message for the World Day of Peace
spells out the political consequences of our destruction of nature when
the Pope suggests that

"World peace is threatened not only by the arms race, regional
conflicts and continued injustices among peoples and nations, but
also by a lack of due respect for nature, by the plundering of
natural resources, and by a progressive decline in the quality of
life."

This study book opened with two things: the Trinity Prayer and a
discussion of a theology through which we might, as Christians,
understand our place and purpose within the will of God. Both
stressed, in a way which would have been unusual even ten years ago,
the importance of creation as being the starting point and purpose of
God. Thus the Trinity Prayer opens with a picture of God as 'Architect
and Innovator, Creator of all from nothing, Source of power,' and
then, 'Parent of humanity'. The image of the Holy Spirit is likewise
powerfully orientated to creation. 'Breath of life' . . . 'who, though
present throughout creation, is particularly close to us here.'

Creation Theology

At the Malvern Conference, from which this book springs, group after group came back to the need for a proper grounding of Christianity in a creation theology. In the plenaries, discussions and worship of the event, time and time again it was creation and the environment which were the focus of people's concern, both theologically, liturgically and practically. As you go further into the implications, political, social, economic, theological and in terms of our responsibilities as citizens and as Christians, you can see why the call for theology to be grounded in a proper theology of creation has arisen. It lies at the very heart of what we think we are here for, what we can really afford to do and how we need to plan for the future. The environment, God's creation, is the very context within which all other aspects of human life and activity have their place. This is why ecological issues are now affecting and influencing all aspects of society.

In our Creed we state that God is the creator of all things, in heaven and on earth, of all things seen and unseen, yet there is little evidence that we have really acted as if we believed this. Over the last ten years Christians have become aware of just how threatened the world of God's creation really is by human activity. Can we defend economic systems which simply see nature as a collection of raw resources? Can we defend an ethos which says that human needs outweigh at all times the needs of the rest of creation? Can we continue to vote for governments which promise us more and more in the way of material benefits, but which do not seem to know how this is going to be achieved without further destruction of the environment?

The Environment

The statistics are all there for us to study: over 10,000 species a year are dying out because of human interference; over half the rain forests of the world destroyed and not renewed within the last forty years; chemicals used for pest control are now found in the bodies of all living creatures on the earth; soil erosion is threatening over 40% of agricultural land in Asia and one third of such land in the USA; global warming is threatening vast tracts of low lying land such as East Anglia, Bangladesh and thousands of island communities.

But such figures often seem to be beyond our real comprehension. For

Christians, the issue is capable of being put more bluntly. God's creation is dying, and we are primarily responsible for this.

In 1988, the BBC in conjunction with WWF and HRH Prince Philip, broadcast a new liturgy for Advent from St. George's Chapel, Windsor. The new liturgy contained a series of poem/laments based on the four candles of Advent. The idea came from a text in Isaiah 48 verses 12 – 13. In this God speaks of having laid the foundations of the earth and spread out the heavens. Isaiah then pictures God calling to all creation and 'they all come forth together'. This idea of God calling forth the elements of creation was developed into The Processions of the Air; the Water; the Land and the Creatures. Here are passages from two of these Processions:

> "Lord, I the Air come.
> Breath of life,
> Wind that moves over the face of the deep.
> Bearing rain,
> I come.
>
> Now the breath of life
> blows death.
> As I pass over the land
> the broken soil follows me:
> a billowing shroud of dust.
>
> When the rain falls,
> forests and lakes die.
>
> I come, my Lord.
> But what have your people made of me
> but a shadow,
> a dark, acidic shadow
> of my God-given glory.
> Breathe on your people, breath of God.
> . . . .
>
> From water,
> air
> and land,

we the creatures came forth
at thy command.

From dust you raised us
and in us
planted your life.

Through the ways
of Time
you brought us
to Be.

Now we come
called forth again.
Yet many
can no longer come.
Gone,
gone for ever.

And we,
we who come.
Can we know
our children's
children
will know this world?

So much has gone.
What remains
is so frail.
Free your people
from their ignorance
and selfishness."

The
Environment

(Pages 15 and 18, 'Advent and Ecology',
published by Radio 4 and WWF UK,
Panda House, Weyside Park, Godalming, Surrey GU7 1XR, 1988)

In each of the poem/laments, the element of creation pleads with God to revive within humanity – us – a sense of what we are doing. There is hope, in other words; that through listening to God, we can be awoken from the spell which seems to have us firmly in its grasp: a spell which makes us treat the world as if it were only there for our use and abuse.

---

1. What changes in your local environment have you noticed in the last ten years? What aspects are better, what aspects are worse?

2. What environmental problems are you aware of now that you were not aware of five years ago? In the group, how much do you know about each of these? How would you set about finding out more? Choose a few topics and ask each person to find out about one of them for your next meeting.

3. Make a fifteen minute act of worship which explores your hopes and fears about God's creation. Try to combine different elements such as a Bible reading, new prayers, a familiar hymn etc.

Is God ending the world?

Some people react to the scale of the environmental crisis which confronts us by claiming that this is part of God's purpose; that the physical diminishing of the creation is a sign that God is winding up this world. Others feel that the signs of the death or crippling of so much of nature shows that God has abandoned the world.

God's first Covenant should dismiss such thoughts from the minds of Christians. In Genesis 9, God makes the first ever Covenant. The Covenant is with Noah and with the descendents of Noah. But it is also with all that flies in the skies, lives on the land and swims in the seas. God promises never to destroy again and sets the rainbow in the sky as a sign of this covenant.

So if it is no part of God's plan to destroy vast tracts of creation, what are we to understand about the environmental crisis and the challenge which it places before Christians? Is there actually a crisis in the first place?

Humans have been affecting the environment ever since we could deliberately create fire, and in particular, ever since we moved from hunter-gathering to agriculture. The over-use of resources was being commented on by writers such as Plato in 4th century BC Athens and by Mencius the sage, in 4th to 3rd century BC China. Both of them complained about deforestation on the hills surrounding major cities. The Sahara desert was once the richest and most fertile farmlands of the Roman Empire, providing most of the grain necessary to sustain the vast cities of Alexandria, Constantinople and Rome itself. Over-farming, loss of control of the lands by local farmers to mega-agricultural organisations in the late Roman Empire and poor fertilising policies led to the creation of a dust bowl. This dust bowl is now spreading rapidly south into other formerly fertile areas.

There is strong evidence that many great civilisations of the past, such as the city states of North India of the 8th to 3rd centuries BC, or the Mayan cities of South America, collapsed because they over-used their natural environment. Those areas of Europe occupied by the Romans also suffered from overexploitation by the Romans and when the Roman empire collapsed, it left many areas with badly damaged ecosystems. It was the Benedictines who revived much of the farm land of Europe through a careful policy of restoring the fertility of the land, tree planting and rotating crop systems which allowed the land time to rest and recover between use.

The Environment

So, at one level, we in Britain have been through a minor ecological crisis before and it was Christianity which largely helped us to recover an understanding of the balance necessary between human use and the needs of the environment. What we have never had to contend with before, nor has anywhere else in the world, is a crisis of such global proportions. The collapse of the Roman Empire, or the North Indian civilisations or the South American cultures, did not have lasting effects on other areas of the world. This is no longer the case. Acid rain created by the vast amounts of chemicals which we pump into the atmosphere in the UK, falls on Sweden and Norway, killing, according to 1988 figures, up to fifty per cent of the forests in Norway and over 20,000 lakes in Sweden. The fall-out from Chernobyl in Russia is still affecting sheep in Cumbria.

The rise in temperature due to greenhouse gases and the increasing of the ozone hole in the atmosphere means that actions such as driving our cars or using CFCs affects lands on the other side of the globe from us. The demand for wood has reduced vast tracts of primal forest to near desert conditions and overfishing of the seas means that many species are close to complete collapse because the nets we use catch everything, leaving no survivors to breed.

It is the global dimension that is the new factor. For there are forces unleashed which we have only just begun to appreciate and it is only by a major change in our attitudes that we shall be able to find a way out of the crisis we have created. Although God promised never to destroy the earth, he never promised to prevent us doing so. Nonetheless, there are some encouraging signs that we are showing increased responsibility. The European Community has made great strides forward in basic environmental protection legislation – legislation which has helped force the UK government to undertake environmental programmes which it otherwise would not have done. But while this is encouraging, there is still an underlying trend towards greater consumption which is fueling the abuse of the natural world.

---

4. Why do you think human societies have always tended to overuse and abuse the environment?

5. What can the Christian faith offer to counteract this tendency?

6. Some people believe that evolution will continue even if human beings destroy themselves; others believe that this may be part of God's plan. How do these two different views affect your view of the environmental crisis?

The witness of the Bible

For Christians, the key to understanding the way God wishes us to live in the world is to be found in the Bible. There, in the opening chapters of Genesis; in many of the psalms such as Psalm 8, 104 and 148; in Job 38 to 39 and in many places in the prophets, we see that God is creator of all and revels in the diversity and beauty of creation. Creation is an outworking of God's very nature as creator and as such creation wishes to give thanks and praise to the Creator. Paul's Letter to the Colossians chapter 1:15 – 20, shows that Jesus Christ came to bring new life and new meaning not just for humanity but for all creation. The Covenant with Noah and with all life on earth sets the scene for God's redemptive work on earth. God's love is for all things on earth – 'For God so loved the world (cosmos – meaning all life) that he sent his only Son'. (John 3:16). St. John also assures us that 'God sent his Son into the world, not to condemn the world, but so that through him the world might be saved.' (3:17.).

Yet, in the past, much Christian, especially Protestant, theology and action has assumed that the incarnation of God in Jesus Christ was a purely human event and that salvation was for us and us alone. The rest of creation has often seemed to be considered little more than a colourful backdrop against which the drama of human salvation was played out. There is a tension within traditional theology about this which needs to be explored if we are to understand both our place within creation and our role in terms of responding to the environmental crisis.

The Environment

The Bible is quite clear about the specialness of humanity. While we are part of the overall creation, we are also clearly apart from the rest of creation. Genesis 1 pictures God setting man and woman upon the earth with dominion over all creatures. In recent years, some Christians have tried to explain away this image of dominion, of being the masters of all living creatures. They have felt that this image of dominion has led us to exploit the world and to treat it as if we and we alone were in charge. It is felt that this attitude has led us to disregard the rest of nature and to set ourselves up as petty tyrants. But we cannot avoid the fact that the Bible very clearly pictures humanity as being special. The issue is not how to get rid of this specialness, but rather, how do we understand this specialness.

There is no question about our being different; no other species on earth has as much impact upon the rest of creation as we do. In what we eat, how we travel, what we build, where we cut down, how we drain and what we kill, we affect nature. Our impact is not always negative, nor are cities to be seen as some ghastly mistake! In many ways, human beings have enriched the diversity of the world. This is a manifestation of our creativity – our being made in the image of God. But we have also exacted a terrible toll on the natural world. So how can we live with the fact that we are so powerful and the fact that so much of what we do is endangering parts of or even the whole of creation?

---

7. The Bible is ambiguous about cities. The first city mentioned is built by Cain (Genesis 4:17). The final vision of the Bible is of the Holy City in Revelation 21:1 – 22:2. In the light of these two passages, discuss your understanding of the city within God's creation, and what it tells us about our role in creation.

Masters, stewards or 'priests'?

Three models of our relationship with nature are offered by different traditions within Christianity and a study of each of these may help us to evolve our own understanding of where we fit into creation and what role we should play.

The first has already been mentioned. It is the role of master of creation, of having dominance. As we have said, in many ways this accurately expresses the present reality but it does so with no moral or ethical consideration. Christians must look at this term and see what moral, ethical and spiritual meaning dominance or mastery should have.

The first thing to say is that any such mastery or domination by Christians has to be seen within the overall mastership of God. Any place or power we have is from God and we are not at the centre of creation, God is. Thus phrases such as 'The Earth is the Lord's and the fulness thereof' (Psalm 24:1) or the prayer at the offertory in the Anglican Holy Communion which says:

"Yours, Lord, is the greatness, the power, the glory, the splendour and the majesty; for everything in heaven and on earth is yours.
All things come from you and of your own do we give you."

remind us that God is the source of all life and that we own nothing, for all belongs to God. Therefore, any mastery or dominion we have is from God and we are responsible to God for the exercise of that power. It is not, as some have claimed, a carte blanche to do as we want with creation. It is more like a vice-regent of a mighty ruler, who is given charge of a part of the empire, but who must answer before the ruler for his actions. And it may be that in picturing God as a mighty ruler, we have sometimes lost a sense of his loving care for creation.

Viewed in this light, what we do to the natural world should be to enhance its diversity and its beauty, for surely God does not want us to diminish what has been created. Yet so often this idea has led us to exploit the world. Indeed, some within the environmental movements point to this idea of dominion and mastery and say that this is why we are in the environmental mess we are in. By thinking that we could act like gods and take and manipulate without thought, we have brought ourselves to the edge. We saw the effects of some of this manipulation in science and technology in the previous chapter. Whatever we think the theology should have been, there is sadly strong evidence to show that we have indeed acted as if we were the sole reason for the rest of creation to exist. We have abused our position of power and have failed to care for creation.

The second image is that of the steward. In many ways, this is a refine- ment of the mastery/dominance model. Like that model, stewardship assumes as central the notion of humanity being apart from the rest of creation. So just as a steward oversees the goods of his or her master or mistress, so we have been set to have oversight over creation. The image of steward also assumes that such a person looks to ensure that nothing runs out, nothing is worn away without being replaced, nothing is done which might damage the integrity of the household

The
Environment

and its smooth running. Indeed this image of a household is central to the steward image and derives from the Greek origin of the words ecology, ecumenical and economics. All three words have as their common root the Greek word for household. Thus economics is about managing the household; ecology is about the nature of the household and ecumenical means to be concerned with all the inhabitants of the household. Over time, all three have also taken on a world wide meaning, rather than just a domestic one.

In this setting, the word steward finds a natural niche. It offers us a vision of the faithful servant who ensures that the household runs smoothly and never overspends or uses up that which it needs to continue. The frequent use of the image of the steward in Jesus's parables reinforces this model. In such Christian use of the stewardship model, it is of course God's household that we are called to be stewards of and in whose service we will find fulfilment. Such a view raises for us the question of whether the way we currently run the world could in any sense be seen as being good stewards. Rather the reverse seems to be the case. The Biblical image which comes to mind for the way we use up resources like oil is that of the foolish virgins in Jesus's parable in Matthew 25, but without the ability to refill our lamps!

To steward the resources of the world for human needs is a challenge which we are struggling to rise to at present. It is even more challenging to be asked to consider our role to be that of stewarding the resources of God's household for the benefit of all creation. It is an aspect of stewardship which is rarely considered, and if it is not considered, the stewardship becomes similar to mastery. It emphasises right use of nature, but not care of nature as such.

These two models stress our responsibility to God and thus our need to use creation wisely. The third model actually shifts the understanding of our special role. It asks us to consider that we might be not masters or stewards, but a source of Blessing to creation. The idea comes from the Orthodox Church and they use the image of the priest. This is not an image which everyone in the churches in the UK is comfortable with, but bear with it for a moment. The following text comes from the Ecumenical Patriarch of Constantinople's major statement on 'Orthodoxy and the Ecological Crisis'.

"We know that as all is from God – as is revealed for instance in Job 38-39 – we must respect creation and acknowledge that we are not its owners, but the ones who may enhance it by use of our technology and skill, only however so as to offer it again to its creator . . . Just as the priest at the Eucharist offers the fullness of creation and receives it back as the blessing of Grace in the form of the consecrated bread and wine, to share with others, so we must be the channel through which God's grace and deliverance is shared with all creation. The human being is simply yet gloriously the means for the expression of creation in its fullness and the coming of God's deliverance for all creation."

This idea of being a channel between God and the rest of creation, being a source of blessing and of opening all creation to its own potential, is a radically different understanding of the uniqueness of humanity in creation. For many it offers a more wholistic approach, placing as much importance on the fullness of all creation as it does on the fulfilment of human potential.

It is important to take some time to explore these three models. Christians need to find a proper place for themselves and for humanity in general within a world created and loved by God. Unless we can articulate a vision of where we belong and what God wishes us to do in relationship to the rest of Creation, we run the risk of continuing to treat the world in such a way that we actually diminish or destroy the God-given glory of creation.

The
Environment

From these theological issues let us now turn to look at the issues which confront us and to ask whether these models can be of help in assisting us to resolve them.

Turn to questions
on next page

8. Think about your local area, and find examples where human beings have acted as
   a) a master
   b) a steward
   c) a blessing.

9. Try to think of other possible models or ways of describing our relationship to the rest of creation. For example, a friend.

10. Explore the language that is used in relation to the land or natural things. For example, people talk of 'conquering' a mountain, 'exploiting' a forest, or on the other hand, 'feeding' a plot of land. What other examples can you think of, and what does this indicate about our society's view of nature?

Development and the environment

Development inevitably means change and change usually means the loss of something that was there before. You cannot develop the industrial base of a country without using up raw materials, building on land, and utilizing resources such as water and energy which means that something has to go. Something is destroyed in order to make the building of factories and homes or the development of farmland possible. Some people in the environmental movement feel that we should not develop anything more; this is a very extreme position held by a very few. But it is an understandable view. Population is placing a terrible strain on the environment and on species.

Although the problem is most visible in the Third World, where increasing population is clearly putting stress on the environment, the real problem is the West's population. An average person in the UK uses up over fifteen times as much of the world's resources as does an average person living in, say, Chad. While there is a great need to reduce the population explosion in many countries, there is also a need to reduce the enormous impact of the population of Europe on the planet. Our consumerist wants are costing the earth. As was pointed out in chapter three, the possibility that Eastern Europe's 250 million citizens might also arrive at comparable consumption levels within the next ten to fifteen years, is very alarming. The planet cannot afford for this to happen.

So what do we do about development? A key phrase in the present debate between development groups and environmental groups is *sustainable development*. This phrase comes from the Bruntland Report prepared for the United Nations. It looks to development being able to proceed in such a way as to use resources that can be regrown or recreated or recycled. This is a very difficult goal to attain. It would mean that we in the West would have to accept a lower standard of living, because elements of our lifestyle are unsustainable. This would touch most powerfully on restricting use or reducing the need for, private transport – the car. It would affect the use of farm-lands for housing and the use of currently wild areas for agriculture. It would affect the energy demands we make and in particular the sorts of fuels we use to make energy.

None of these are comfortable ideas. But they are issues which have to be faced if the messages the environment is sending us are to be heeded and actions taken to stop the degrading of our environment. Those wishing to be a blessing to nature will have to take on board something of the suffering and pain of creation by self-denial in order that other species may be able to live. The Pope has called for a 'culture of asceticism' in order to save the planet.

---

11. In the light of the last paragraph, and the question of equal opportunities for development, what needs changing in your life? What organisations or groups would help you in this? What role could the Church play?

God as creator and sustainer

In spite of our efforts, we are bombarded by worrying data about problems which make us feel powerless, and by talk of destruction and the end of the world. In this situation, Christians need to hold even more firmly to the image of God as both creator and sustainer. As Christians, we have to believe that the structures of society can be changed, can be converted, from the ways which lead to exploitation and into the ways that lead to life. Again, we come back to the question of whether Christianity has an adequate vision of the transformation of structures rather than just the redemption and salvation of individuals. This issue, raised in earlier chapters is equally relevant here. Christians have been very good at responding to the request to recycle. Many churches collect newspaper – even if it is with half an eye on a few extra pounds for the church roof! Many church youth groups or organisations have made ecology part of their work and service in their area. But the question remains. Can we find a vision of the transformation of our consumption led society towards one in which needs are met, but wants are restrained? Do we have a theology of social and structural change which will enable us as Christians, as inhabitants of our country and as citizens of the wider world, to play our part in reshaping society for the benefit of all creation?

"MUM WHAT CHANNEL IS GOD ON?"

WHAT MEDIUM?
WHAT MESSAGE?
ARTS, EDUCATION AND MEDIA

It is said that when the tsar of the newly formed Russian state which emerged in the late 10th century, was looking to the future, he wanted a proper religion for his new nation. At that time the Russians had a mixture of different beliefs. So he sent an embassy to visit the two great religious centres and faiths of the world. These were Islam, centred on Baghdad and Orthodox Christianity based on Constantinople.

The Embassy went first to Baghdad. There they observed the unity which Islam brought; they were impressed by the regular prayer times and the fact that everyone obeyed them; they listened to the Islamic law being propounded; they were very impressed by this faith which seemed so ordered and clear about its priorities. They wrote a long report to the tsar extolling the virtues of Islam and suggesting that this was the faith Russia should embrace. They requested that they be allowed to return home, saying that visiting Constantinople was no longer necessary.

The tsar commanded them to fulfill the original mandate of the embassy, and so, grudgingly, they travelled on to Constantinople. They arrived and were immediately taken to Hagia Sophia, the great church of Holy Wisdom which still dominates the city. As they entered, the eucharistic liturgy reached its climax and the music resounded from the mosaics, icons and frescoes of the church. In their report the members of the embassy wrote *We did not know whether we were in heaven or on earth.*. On the strength of that sublime experience, the tsar decided in favour of Christianity and the Russian **98** Orthodox Church was born, in 988 AD.

The Church – patron of the arts

The interaction between art and faith is one which in the past, Christianity has excelled at. The great churches and monasteries bear witness to the extraordinary skills, devotion and artistic excellence which Christianity could call forth from people. The builders and craftspeople who built these great buildings knew that through their art, the Christian faith and its messages would be heard and seen for centuries to come. The Church seems to have understood the relationship between medium and message very well. It drew upon the full range of artistic skills and media of communication that were to hand: music, architecture, dance, drama, paintings, frescoes, mosaics, sculpture, song, symbolism, the written word, the spoken word and so forth to broadcast the teachings and stories of the faith.

In doing so it seems to have integrated the arts with education, expressing the core values which underpinned the world of Christendom.

The Trinity Prayer reminds us that this is an aspect of the work of the Father, Son and Holy Spirit. The Prayer speaks of God as 'Architect and Innovator'. Jesus is praised as the 'Storyteller' while the Holy Spirit is the 'Lamplighter' – the one who lights up the world and shows us the way. The image of God as creator architect is central to the Old Testament understanding of God. The images which are used to describe God's relationship with that which is created are of the potter working with clay; the architect laying out the foundations; the craftsperson creating the loving details. God's creativity is a vital part of that image which is found reflected in all of us. There is no question but that Christianity has a positive vision of God as artist and creator.

Jesus is an artist in another sense. His mastery of the art of storytelling is obvious to anyone who knows the parables or who reads the stories of how Jesus taught. Jesus paints pictures in words and draws us into the drama of what he has to say through the details and intimacy of the stories. In recent years, theology has rediscovered the art of storytelling – of what is called 'narrative theology'. We have discovered what many people have known for a long time. That the story of God's love for the world, the story of the Exodus, of Jesus's own life and his stories, speak eternally to people. The Biblical story can become their story as

Education and Media

they come to understand what is happening to them through the medium of the Bible stories. Take the great songs of the American slaves, where they tell of their plight using the imagery and metaphors of the Bible. In more recent days, liberation theology has shown how the Bible story speaks loud and clear to oppressed people in South America.

To return to the picture of the ancient church building, this was often a superb mixture of materials, skills and artistic traditions which fused together to convey one overarching value – the centrality of the Christian faith to the community which created the building. Such a building might well be a mixture of two or more styles. The carvings will probably mix pre-Christian gods and demons with angels and scenes of local characters getting drunk or having their tooth pulled. The paintings will depict the major events of the Bible in settings from the local area and in the costumes of the time. But through all this mixture comes the one clear message of the vitality of the Christian faith. Art, architecture and community seem to be of one intent if of different traditions and skills..

3. Look at the opening story about the tsar's ambassadors. If they came now, to your church during a service, what would their report be?

4. What is your favourite Bible story? What is the most memorable way you have ever heard it told?

The loss of coherence

Europe today is no longer coherent in this way. It has not been so for a long time. For much of the previous century, this diversification was taken as a sign of the maturation and development of Europe from its own historic past. The diversification of art, of culture in its broadest sense, and of values, was seen as an important part of overthrowing the forced uniformity of thought which the Church had imposed on the artistic and intellectual skills of Europe. In many ways this was true and we need to remember how important the diversification of values, culture and arts has been. Our societies today would be the poorer without the development of the novel, modern dance, early industrial architecture such as the suspension bridge, and without the means of modern mass communication including the radio, TV and the introduction of new cultures into our social and artistic life.

Diversity is however a mixed blessing. It offers us the chance of liberty and freedom, but it also threatens our sense of being part of one culture. In recent years, much concern has been expressed about the eroding of the common culture of Britain, or of Europe. While much of this is often essentially reactionary in nature – a fear or disdain for anything new – there is also a growing concern that we are in danger of falling apart for lack of any substantial undergirding values which can act as a bedrock on which we build. The growth in new religious and ethnic communities within Europe – Islam, Hinduism, Afro-Caribbean for example – are seen by some as posing major questions to our sense of a coherent identity. Alongside this, the growth in alternative lifestyles or values is seen as undercutting the foundational values on which Europe and the family and Christianity are built. Some examples cited are the gay/lesbian movements, breakdown of marriage and the many single parent families, and greater permissiveness in general.

The wish to have a strong, communal sense of belonging, of shared values is deep-seated. We like to believe that what we are doing is right and is what our forebears did. Tradition is of immense importance to people – even when the traditions are quite recent! We like to feel that we are part of a continuum. The revival in interest in 18th century architectural styles is as much a search for tradition and a sense of belonging as it is a reaction against the brutalism of much modern architecture.

Education and Media

The sense of belonging

There is a story told of a Visigoth king who was converted by a missionary bishop in the 6th century AD, somewhere deep in the forests of Germany. As was the fashion in those days, the bishop blessed a local river and the Visigoth king drove all his people, many thousands of them, through the river. They entered as pagans and emerged as baptised Christians. If the king was to become a Christian, then everyone else had to be in the same camp of faith as well. However, that night the king threw a great party. Late in the evening, far gone in his cups, the king leaned across to the missionary bishop and commented; "How wonderful it will be in heaven, when I, the king, can feast again with all my beloved ancestors and the fallen heroes of my youth". The bishop looked scandalised and pointed out; "Your fallen friends and ancestors died as pagans and so will be down in hell, not up in heaven!". Aghast, the king thought for a few moments and then rose from the table. He ordered all his people to return to the river. There, he drove them back through the waters and returned them to their former pagan selves. He had decided that he would rather be in hell with his friends and ancestors than alone in heaven!

The sense of belonging and community which seems to have motivated the Visigoth king is one which is still strong today. Not many people would actually be as extreme in their response as the king, but many of us no doubt feel at times that we are, as a society, drifting away from anything which can really be said to bind us together with those around us, those who have gone before and those who will come after.

As Britain moves closer to the rest of Europe and as diversity becomes yet more and more an acknowledged part of our society, what is the role of the Church and of Christians in the shaping of values in our society? Can there actually be any constructive role for Christianity, which having been for so long the cornerstone of European culture, is now either ignored by large sections of society or is seen as one amongst a number of different views which make up our wider society? Can the Church, which itself seems split over values and education, the role of art and of media, offer any insights into the ways in which values can be expressed and held in a pluralist society such as ours?

5. In this group,
a) How important is it to you that you are a member of a particular church tradition or denomination?
b) Is your family part of the same tradition? Whether you answer yes or no, how does that affect your membership of your family and your membership of your church?
c) How far does your church make you feel part of an international community, and does this affect your sense of being British?

6. Read Joshua 24:1-24. Is Joshua building a religious community, a national community, or both? To what extent do stories of the past affect your sense of belonging to particular groups (family, nation, Europe, etc)? How do you continue the stories with new members of the community?

7. What is your reaction to religious and cultural diversity?

The arts and Christianity today

At the Malvern Conference of 91, Murray Watts, the playwright, raised the issue of the role of the arts in contemporary Christianity. He pleaded for a positive attitude towards those working in the arts and in media who were trying to express the Gospel in new ways and through new media. The reception given to his appeal was enthusiastic and he was warmly applauded. Yet the fact remained that, with the sole exception of the liturgies and worship, no other form of communication was used at the Conference than words, written or spoken. It is true that the conference was set up mainly for people to talk to each other, but maybe this captures the sad decline in Christianity's involvement in any substantial way with the arts. Is it significant that the only place where alternative forms of communication were used was in the section of the conference set aside for 'young people'? While some magnificent art has been created for new churches – such as the work of Piper at Coventry Cathedral or Chagal for Chichester Cathedral – Christianity, once the powerhouse of sponsorship and imagery for

Education and Media

103

art, now finds it difficult to compete with the power of popular images presented by our culture.

While there are a growing number of Catholics, Britain is mainly Protestant, with a predominantly Protestant culture. As such, the church has inherited a tremendous emphasis on the Word as being the means by which truth is imparted. The Protestant revolution was founded upon the Bible and on making the Bible accessible to all people. The Word, read, preached and printed, was what fueled and fed the rise of the Protestant churches and they were deeply suspicious of any other form of communication such as art. The destruction of the statues and wall paintings in our churches during periods of Protestant fanaticism was not just an attack on the old Roman Catholic beliefs. It was an attack on art itself and an assertion of the supremacy of the Word. Likewise, the dislike of liturgy and symbol – elements of Christian life which are so central in Roman Catholic or Orthodox worship – was manifest in the destruction of the altars and the forbidding of vestments. Look at the central object in a Roman Catholic church and in a Gospel hall or Baptist chapel. In the Roman Catholic church, it will be the altar. In the Gospel Hall or Baptist chapel, it will be the pulpit and/or lectern. The Word is supreme.

This emphasis on the Word has meant that much of contemporary Protestant Christianity is uncomfortable with art and with the ambiguities of art – be that drama, dance or painting. This has meant that there is little of a tradition for many in the churches to draw upon in terms of an appreciation of the role of art in either our churches or in society at large. Hence its absence from an event such as Malvern 91 – or indeed from almost any major church gathering anywhere, with the limited exception of Greenbelt which is primarily concerned with music.

It is therefore hard to see what sort of role Christianity can play in the arts and in values in the arts, for it really has little contemporary experience to build upon. However, many within the arts are only too aware of the role they play in expressing, often in ways far beyond the power of words, those insights and truths which help us shape our lives – many of which come from Christianity. Many artists and writers are themselves Christians and seek through their work to explore the relationship of the faith to contemporary issues and media. But they receive little in the way of support or recognition from the institutions of the churches.

---

8. Read Ezekiel 12:1-7. God pushed Ezekiel into dramatic expression of his message. What would be an equivalent today?

9. Look at your own life. For most of us, our appreciation of the Christian faith will have come from a variety of influences – people, places, crises, events, hymns, songs, stories and so forth. Discuss the ways in which art – in the form of music, dance, song, painting, drama or some other form – has helped shape your faith and your understanding of the meaning of your faith.

10. Based on your discussions, make a collage of your sources of inspiration. You could use an old roll of wallpaper as the mount, and collect magazines, pictures, glue, scissors. Some can paint or draw while others can use pictures etc. cut out from magazines to make their contribution. Give each person a share of the paper space (about two feet of space per person), but try to make them link up. Be prepared for a lot of mess, but a lot of fun!

Who pays the piper?

To what extent can society assume that the arts will reflect its values? In the past, when the Church was the paymaster, art supported the Christian vision. That has long since ceased to be the case and is part of the broadening out of society and its values mentioned earlier. Artists have often been innovators of developments within our culture. Even when the church was the paymaster, they took the faith into new areas and into new forms of expression – but not always with the church's blessing!

Nowadays, much art is commercial. The image of artists struggling away in their attic is a popular idea, but one which bears little relationship to the current situation of the employment of artistic skills in such industries as advertising, architecture, commercially commissioned

Education
and
Media

paintings or even illustrations for books! Like science, much art has become consumer driven and guided in that the major funders are looking for images that speak about their importance not the importance of art as such. This is really not that much different from the days when the church employed the craftspeople and artists. It just means that there are now many different groups using the artist's talents. Much of this is to promote values of consumerism and the contentment which is supposed to arise from consumerism. For example, more artists work in advertising than in any other way.

There are of course those who create regardless of the economic necessities of life. There are artists who work with an immense integrity and who explore many different themes. But the usual art encountered by ordinary people, be it in the form of paintings of happy families on cornflake packets or corporation art in the foyer of the headquarters, or the latest form of modern architecture, is essentially commercially driven and as such probably almost as cohesive as the older church driven art and architecture. So it may be that what concerns people about contemporary art is not so much that art does not offer us a set of values we can identify with, but that in fact much of it does. The trouble is that we may be at heart a little dissatisfied with the values of consumerism and free-enterprise 'happiness' culture.

The role of the Church in this is surely to seek to encourage the development of alternatives to much of the contemporary use of art and craftspeople's skills. We cannot fund in the way that the medieval church could, but we can encourage and seek to ensure that the creative be much more part and parcel of our ways of working and reflecting. We could invite artists to reflect for us on the contemporary meaning of Christianity for our age.

This could mean we run risks. In 1990, for example, the World Wide Fund for Nature (WWF) invited young people to create a painting or some other artistic form to express the idea of 'The suffering of God's creation', for a festival of Christianity and ecology in Salisbury Cathedral. WWF funded the venture, but the church provided the stimulus. The winning painting was extraordinary and disturbing. It showed a beautiful Amazonian bird of paradise, crucified upon a cross, with its head inclined at the traditional angle that Christ's head is given in the great paintings of the crucifixion.

Some people were worried that the painting might give offence, but eventually agreed to let it be shown. The effect on the thousands of visitors to the festival was dramatic. No-one passed it by without looking more closely. Many stood for a long time reflecting on the painting. Many were moved to come and discuss its meaning with those on duty and this discussion almost always led to a religious discussion about the meaning of the death and resurrection of Christ as a sign of hope for the whole world. That one painting probably communicated more about the relationship between the Christian faith and the fate of the world than did any of the lectures or sermons preached that weekend.

It is not only the church that is expected to communicate values. This demand is also made of education and the mass media. At times of identity crisis or of changing values, both these groups come in for attack as well as for almost impossible expectations.

11. Look at television, magazine or poster advertisements. Take one and ask:
a) What values is it communicating?
b) What values is it appealing to?

12. Do you think the church should use the power of advertising? Would the medium clash with the message?

13. Advertising agencies recently took part in a competition organised by their association (not sponsored by the church!) in which they designed advertising campaigns to encourage church attendance. One of the winning entries said 'Terry Waite cannot be in church today. What's your excuse?'
a) What emotions or values does this appeal to?
b) Taking other church publicity and 'wayside pulpits', what values and emotions do they appeal to?
c) How would you attract people to Christianity through the media?

Education and Media

Education and values

Education is one of the few areas that just about everyone feels entitled to have a view on. After all, most of us went to school for ten to eleven years. We know what goes on and what ought to go on! This is rather like the problem which Mrs. Golda Meir reported on when she was Prime Minister of Israel. She is said to have commented that she ruled a country of over three million prime ministers, each one of whom knew he or she could do it better than her!

Society places great expectations on the shoulders of education. In 1981 when there were riots in several inner cities, a government minister in the Education Department commented that this was a sign of the failure not just of education, but of religious education in particular. Education is the place where the changes in society tend to have their earliest and most direct impact. The growth of new religious and ethnic communities in Britain has led to the rise of multi-cultural and multi-faith education. Recognition of the special needs of people with learning difficulties has led to the rise of special education. The increased difficulties of the family unit have meant that many teachers have to carry heavy pastoral duties on top of their teaching load.

However, education itself is also in something of a crisis. It reflects a plurality of values about how to teach and, even with the national curriculum, what to teach, which mirrors the difficulties in identity and common values in the wider society. Some people believe that education should be imparting the common values, the firm foundation on which society can build. But this is impossible for education can only ever, as an overall system, deliver that which the society actually values and believes itself.

Church schools

This pluralism of values and uncertainty about direction is reflected in the attitude of the Church to its own schools, not just in Britain but in many parts of Europe. Christianity has had a long and honourable involvement with education. The model of Jesus as teacher has profoundly influenced Christianity and has given education and the teacher a high status.

Two models of education operated within Christianity until very recently. The first was the missionary model. Education was developed to help a people new to the faith to grasp both its importance and its vision of reality. Thus the Orthodox Church when seeking to convert areas such as Bulgaria in the 9th to 10th centuries, saw the establishment of educational centres and the creation of an alphabet (the Cyrillic script) as essential in the task of conversion. At roughly the same time, King Alfred the Great of Wessex was establishing schools as a vital part of his policy of unifying the people under Christianity. In the massive missionary movement of the 19th century, schools and colleges were amongst the major institutions established by mission boards in new areas such as Africa and Asia.

The second model has been that of the consolidation and development of the Christian society. The universities founded across Europe from the 12th century onwards and the schools established by kings of England such as Henry VI, were designed to impart Christian truths and to provide a place where the Christian leadership could be trained for both religious and secular roles in life. When the idea of education for the working class was first being developed at the end of the 18th and beginning of the 19th century, Christians were foremost in their support for they saw that if the working class could be educated into the values of the Christian society, then revolutions such as the French had experienced would not take place.

But what is our model today? The vision of converting the world in one generation is gone, so what has happened to the missionary dimension of Christian involvement in education in Europe? Many of the teachers in church schools will reflect a diversity of views on just about every topic, the same diversity as is found not just in society, but also within the Church. Few people would still argue that Britain, or indeed large sections of northern Europe can any longer be described as Christian societies. Therefore, the second role of sustaining the Christian culture is no longer really relevant. There is a real crisis of identity for Church schools across northern Europe which reflects the difficulties which secular schools also face.

Schools, whether Christian in origin, or secular, are trying to reflect the values of a pluralist world. They seek to ensure that children of

Education and Media

different backgrounds are given a strong sense of their own worth, and of the worth of their home culture. They try to stress the importance of each child and of the child's experience as a vital foundation for learning. The debates in the UK about the content of the National Curriculum have highlighted the desire of many to return to a more formal style of teaching and a more traditional curriculum. Yet in practice, good teachers have always drawn in and built upon the strengths contained within the pupils in their actual class.

Most schools, despite tabloid headlines every so often, are attempting to impart a sense of mutual responsibility and of common decency and consideration to their pupils. These basic values are respected by most communities in this country. What is more controversial is when teachers wish to challenge a very European-centred view of history or of literature. When teachers suggest that great world literature might include Indian literature such as the Ramayana, alongside classic Western books. Or when teachers suggest that teaching about the 'discovery' of America by the West is insensitive to the peoples who were already living there. Then, education touches raw spots in our own identity as a majority people and faith within a society where we feel we are losing ground. Yet Christianity teaches as its foundation, respect and love for different people, and a belief that the foreigner may have much to teach us – as in the story of the Good Samaritan.

Christians need to avoid the common fault of blaming education for reflecting the views and diversity which are to be found in society. Schools can and do offer a place where new ideas and understandings of identity and worth are tried out. Not all of these are successful, but many are. Multi-cultural education has probably contributed more to a growing understanding of diversity and its value in society than any other single initiative. But multicultural education has also been hijacked at times by those with agendas different from education's own – and this relates to the political right as well as the left. Schools try to reflect in practice what many of us know in theory but try to ignore in everyday life: that Britain is an increasingly fragmented society, whose unity can no longer be said to come from just one religious or ideological viewpoint.

14. What role do you think schools can have in preserving or changing values? Does Christianity have a contribution to make to this?

15. How well does your church educate both young people and lay people in general?

16. 'Schools can and do offer a place where new ideas and understanding of identity and worth are tried out.' Should the church also offer this opportunity? If so, in what way? Think about possible use of the arts and drama in this process.

In searching for a new identity, we have to ask who provides the clues to this? Who feeds our imagination or who tells us what is going on? The role of the media in this is a controversial one and again, Christians need to be encouraged to express their faith through the media. It is not enough to set up religious TV stations, which too easily become a sign of a ghetto mentality of retreat from the wider world.

To many outsiders, Britain and Europe seem to have a very clear set of values and a clear goal for our societies: the exploitation of the rest of the world in order that our consumerist lifestyle can continue. The Rev. Jose Chipenda is General Secretary of the All Africa Council of Churches, based in Nairobi, Kenya. To him, Europe has a clear agenda and values which it is pursuing:

> "The signposts guiding Europeans to the future tell us that economic prosperity for the West rather than economic justice for all will prevail. The 'New World Order' favours the haves and rejects the have nots. It is for the mighty and not for the righteous. It gives emphasis on material production and consumption, instead of giving attention to social, mental and spiritual development."
>
> *(Speech given to Malvern Conference 91)*

Education and Media

This may seem rather harsh to many of us, but look at the vision of our society which the media conveys. Our advertisements tell us to buy more and more in order to enjoy 'happiness' and 'security'. The xenophobic nature of many of our newspapers presents a frightening vision of a narrow, insular people – as with The Sun's 'Up yours Delors' campaign. TV is largely filled with material which encourages us to imitate a way of life which sees value in material possessions. Our banking system is showing increasing signs of corruption and of abuse of its power and role in life. The concerns of the vast majority of the world's population – food, housing, welfare and the environment – rarely warrant presentation on the front pages of our papers or in the major news items of the radio or TV news. Taking a critical view of what we tell ourselves about ourselves through our media, it is hard not to agree with Rev. Jose Chipenda.

Yet, once again, the tendency to blame the media for reporting, even if at times in an exaggerated way, what they observe of our society, is unhelpful. Christians need to be able to offer a better vision and perception of life, a greater set of values which can provide a counter-balance to the prevailing values. All too often the voices of the lonely and the marginalised, the unemployed and the poor, tend to get little attention. In programmes like the Church Urban Fund and charities such as CAFOD, Traidcraft or Christian Aid, Christians can bear witness to other values. Values which may run us up against the general values of our society – a society which we once assumed shared our values. This assumption can no longer be made. This is liberating for many Christians for it presents the chance to look long and hard at what we believe society should be like, what our role in Europe should be and our place and responsibility to the rest of the world should be. In the light of these wider considerations, we then need to find those within our society who share our vision, even if they do not share our faith. And together perhaps we can begin to establish a new set of values, which can coherently and practically take its place more firmly within society – possibly even challenging the sort of values which Jose Chipenda sees so strongly presented in his encounter with our society, culture and values.

---

17. In the last paragraph the question of a new vision was raised, not just for the church but for society. Choose one medium that does not use words (painting, mime, dance, music etc.) and use it to explore the meaning and significance of a text such as Matthew 28:20.

PARTNERS IN THE FUTURE

"Behold I am doing a new thing; now it springs forth, do you not perceive it?"

(Isaiah 43:19).

So what of the future? Through the various chapters of this study book and the discussions on the tape, we have looked at some of the pressing social, economic, environmental and technological issues which confront us today. These self-same issues have led some in our world to despair of the future. This however cannot be the attitude of Christians. When the Archbishop of Canterbury opened the Malvern Conference 91, he chose as his text the above quote from Isaiah.

We opened this book with the words of Jesus to his disciples at the Ascension. Jesus has promised to be with us when we do his will, 'even until the end of time.' As Isaiah reminds us, God is the God of change, through which he can make all things new.

Many search for certainty before they are willing to act. The Archbishop of York, also speaking at the Malvern Conference, turned to that great spiritual activist and writer, Simone Weil to help us understand how we need to go into the future. He used a quote from her writings:

"I still half refused (God), not my love but my intelligence. For it seemed to me certain, and I still think so today, that one can never wrestle enough with God if one does so out of pure regard for truth. Christ likes us to prefer truth to him because, before being Christ, he is truth. If one turns aside from him to go towards the truth, one will not go far before falling into his arms."

As Dr. Habgood commented, 'Here in a passion for truth open to find Christ as he makes himself known to us, lies a faith in the future, and for the future.'

We have made frequent reference to the Trinity Prayer which was used at the opening service of the Malvern Conference 91. The Prayer was followed by the following prayer:

"We, paused on the threshold of the future,
uncertain of its shape,

unclear of our role and perhaps tempted
to cling to the seeming certainties of the past;
We, your stewards on earth,
call on you to inspire our thinking,
inform our speaking
and amend our living,
so that through us, in whatever way, the kingdoms of this world
and of this time may be blessed
with the character of heaven
and addressed by the Word of your Son
in whose name we pray."

We need to be reminded that we have a role in the future. The crisis of confidence that has shaken Christianity and the collapsing of other great certainties has left many shaken and unsure. The profound challenge which the environmental crisis or the growth of armaments and their bloody consequences has had on our self-perception has not always been helpful. The tendency to turn aside from the issues of the world towards the intricacies of the world of religion is very strong. Yet we profess a belief in the God who created all life and who so loved this planet that he sent his Son. We believe in Jesus Christ 'who though able to put right the world by decree, saves it by suffering', and we believe in the Holy Spirit 'who, though present throughout creation, is particularly close to us here.'

This chapter is not about the blueprint for a Christian future. It is about the reasons why Christians can hope for the future by taking seriously the challenges and openings for the Gospel and for Christian involvement in every aspect of our contemporary society and with the issues highlighted in the earlier chapters.

This will not be in the form of re-establishing the Church as the sole body of authority in society. Those days are over, as the Archbishop of York spells out:

" . . . there are many conscious of the deep importance of religious faith and deeply suspicious of the churches . . . . I suspect that at least part of what we now call secularisation is not about the loss of inner religious awareness, but about the fear of being trapped by certainties in a religious context, especially one where rather strident forms of certainty seem to be on the increase."

In many ways, the Christian is asked to be active in a world which is now openly pluralist and where the Christian faith has to take its place alongside many other views and attitudes. It is through the nature of its actions and the depth of its spirituality that the Christian faith will speak to the future, not by dint of its historic position or power. It also seems increasingly likely that Christians, while being part of the pluralism which makes up our society, will have to take certain stands against the prevailing ethos of a society which is literally consuming the world and destroying countless lives in the process.

Christianity is sometimes spoken of as being the grandmother of our present culture. The freedom to explore and to use the world which the Bible gives us, has been taken as a right to exploit and abuse. The sense of belonging has been turned into a love of possessions. The understanding of ourselves as having a special place in creation has been replaced by an attitude which puts us at the centre of creation – where God should be. If Christianity is indeed the grandmother, then she has a duty to speak sharply to her grandchildren and to try to show how the values which have been perverted should be lived out. Sadly, she has failed to do this for many years and there are even those in our society who feel she has no right to speak at all. She also needs to reassure and to gently guide her young, in the way that grandmothers can do. And she also needs to listen to what her grandchildren tell her of the world they now inhabit and of the fears and hopes which they have.

As Christians there may seem to be little which we can do, either individually or collectively. But this is not true. Throughout the study chapters there are suggestions of actions which can arise from issues, discussions and activities undertaken as part of this series. As a group, you may well have already decided on one or two of these which you want to follow up. As an individual, you may likewise have found

something which rings a bell for you.

It is important for all of us to find others who care about the issue or who are trying to change things. We cannot always assume that these people will be found within the Churches. We need to look for allies in the wider world. For example, any one wishing to become involved in environmental issues will gain a great deal from the information which a body like WWF has, the campaigning experience of Friends of the Earth or the dramatic tactics of Greenpeace. It is a waste of time for us to try and reinvent the wheel. We can learn from those who, for a variety of different reasons, care about the same issues as ourselves. We can begin to explain to them the particular Christian motivation which has led us to wish to grapple with these issues.

There is one very important attribute which Christians can bring to the issues we have outlined. Celebration. Christians have faith in the future because Christ has promised to walk beside us into that future. Therefore we have hope and hope is a cause for celebration. Let us open our doors as a church to celebrate those things which we all value and enjoy but which we rarely remember to give thanks for. Again, taking an issue like the environment, Christians are involved in ecology because we know that God has created all things and loves all creation. This is a reason to rejoice and be glad in the Lord. Many churches have in recent years held festivals to celebrate the gift of creation. To these they have invited many groups in their community to come and share, bringing their own insights, knowledge and experience of the importance of creation, as well as their hopes and fears. This celebration has given many people within the secular environmental movements a greater sense of hope. So often such people are having to present the gloomy side of our relationship with nature. A chance to celebrate the beauty which is why we mourn its loss, is welcomed by almost everyone. In offering such a chance, Christians are showing hope for the future and offering others an opportunity to see the role of faith in the future.

As Christians, we need to work on understanding what our faith has to say not just to individuals in need of redemption and forgiveness, love and compassion, but what we have to say to institutions which are in a similar need. We are not very good at dealing with structures. We tend to prefer going for the individual. But our world is increasingly

Partners in the Future

119

a collection of powerful structures and as Christians we need to explore that tension of understanding of power structures which lies between Romans 13 and the alternative spelt out in the Book of Revelation as we discussed in chapter 2. Until we have begun to see what Christ has to say to Caesar as well as to Mammon, our witness will be incomplete.

The Malvern Conference of 1991, from which this book and the BBC series 'Faith in the Future' sprang, showed that many Christians are concerned to engage in such questions and to debate the role of the faith in society. Likewise, Malvern also illustrated the vast array of attitudes and beliefs which the Church now has within it. Pluralism is not just something the rest of society has – it is vividly present within our own churches. Many different conclusions will be drawn by people from the issues discussed in this book. We certainly do not expect or want uniformity. But we do hope that as we move forward into the third millenium of Christianity, that the Christian witness will continue to grow and to mature as we look back to our rootedness in the Gospel and forward into the mists of the future. Christianity has profoundly shaped and influenced the last two thousand years. It will in some way shape and affect the next thousand. In what way, lies in our power, by being faithful to the call of the Gospel and manifesting God's love for all creation through our lives and through our faith.

Perhaps there is no better way to end this book than with the famous prayer of St. Theresa:

> "Christ has no body now on earth but ours,
> no hands but ours,
> no feet but ours.
> Ours are the eyes
> through which Christ's compassion looks out on the world;
> ours are the feet by which
> he goes about doing good;
> and ours are the hands with which he blesses people now."

1. Plan a celebration for your community, focussing on one or more of the topics covered in this book. Choose a suitable occasion within the church's year – maybe Harvest Festival or Trinity Sunday, taking account of the Trinity prayer with which the book starts. What groups in the local community could provide input? Decide with them on a focus for your celebration. What specifically Christian input do you want to bring? Create an act of worship celebrating the Christian understanding of your theme.

**Partners
in the
Future**

FURTHER READING

CHAPTER 2 – Whose Society is it Anyway?
Alton, David. *Faith in Britain*. Hodder and Stoughton, 1991.
Field, Frank. *Politics and Paradise*. Fount, 1987.
Temple, William. *Christianity and Social Order*. SPCK, 1942.

CHAPTER 3 – Who Pays for Wealth?
Dorr, Donal. *The Social Justice Agenda*. Gill and MacMillan, 1991.
Robertson, James. *Future Wealth*. Cassells, 1989.
Sider, Ronald. *Rich Christians in an Age of Hunger*. Hodder, 1977.
Walter, Tony. *Hope on the Dole*. SPCK, 1985.

CHAPTER 4 – Masters of the Universe?
Davis, Paul. *The Cosmic Blueprint*. Unwin, 1987.
Moltmann, Jurgen. *Creating a Just Future*. SCM, 1989.
Polkinghorne, John. *One World*. SPCK, 1986.

CHAPTER 5 – New Heaven, New Earth?
Bradley, Ian. *God is Green*. Darton, Longman and Todd, 1990.
Cooper, Tim. *Green Christianity*. Hodder and Stoughton, 1990.
McDonagh, Sean. *The Greening of the Church*. Chapman, 1990.
Orthodoxy and the Ecological Crisis; available from WWF UK, Panda House, Godalming, GU7 IXR.

CHAPTER 6 – What Medium? What Message?
Field, Martin. *Faith in the Media*. Hodder and Stoughton. 1991.
Hull, John. *What Prevents Christian Adults From Learning?* . SCM,1985.
Wright, David, editor. *Essays in Evangelical Social Ethics* Paternoster Press, 1979.